Collins

Year 4
Maths & English
Targeted Study & Practice Book

Jon Goulding and Sarah-Anne Fernandes

How to use this book

This Maths and English Study and Practice book contains everything children need for the school year in one book.

A **study page** and a **practice page** for each topic.

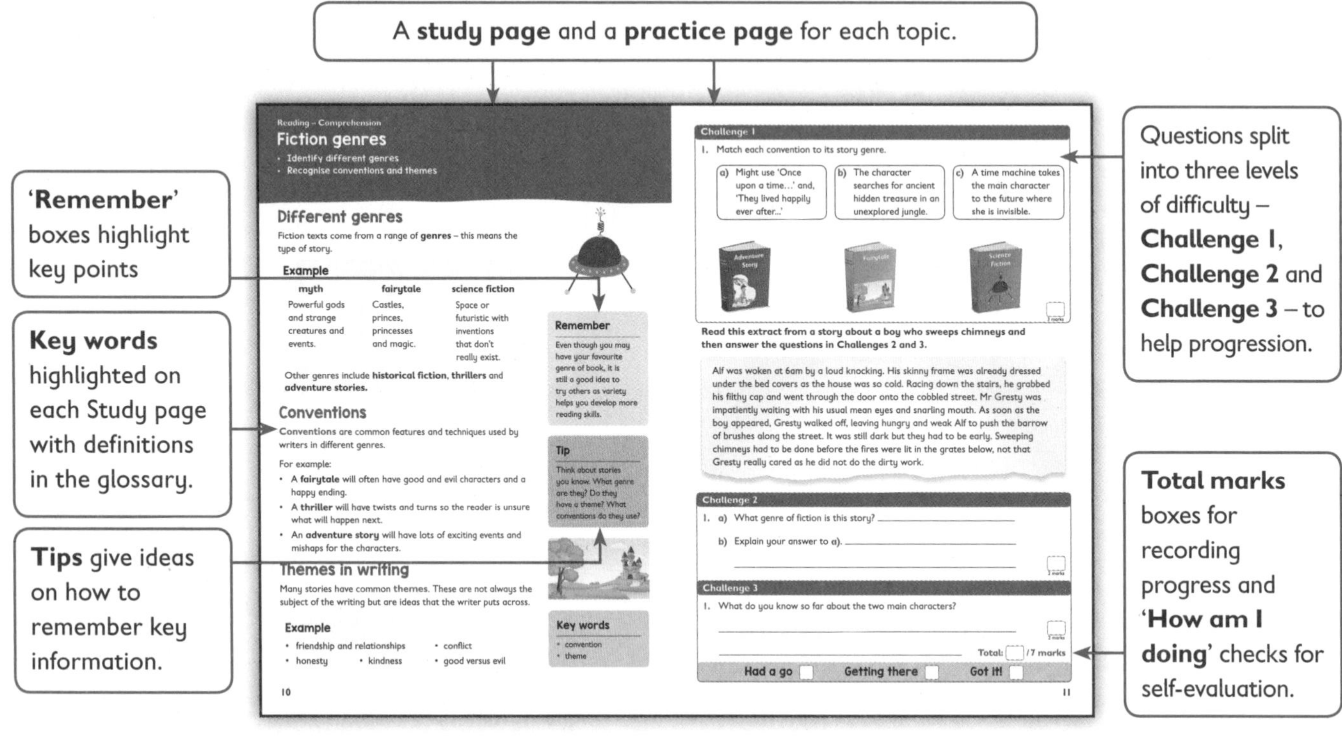

'**Remember**' boxes highlight key points

Key words highlighted on each Study page with definitions in the glossary.

Tips give ideas on how to remember key information.

Questions split into three levels of difficulty – **Challenge 1**, **Challenge 2** and **Challenge 3** – to help progression.

Total marks boxes for recording progress and '**How am I doing**' checks for self-evaluation.

Reading – Comprehension

Fiction genres

- Identify different genres
- Recognise conventions and themes

Different genres

Fiction texts come from a range of **genres** – this means the type of story.

Example

myth	fairytale	science fiction
Powerful gods and strange creatures and events.	Castles, princes, princesses and magic.	Space or futuristic with inventions that don't really exist.

Other genres include **historical fiction**, **thrillers** and **adventure stories**.

Conventions

Conventions are common features and techniques used by writers in different genres.

For example:

- A **fairytale** will often have good and evil characters and a happy ending.
- A **thriller** will have twists and turns so the reader is unsure what will happen next.
- An **adventure story** will have lots of exciting events and mishaps for the characters.

Themes in writing

Many stories have common themes. These are not always the subject of the writing but are ideas that the writer puts across.

Example

- friendship and relationships
- honesty
- kindness
- conflict
- good versus evil

Remember

Even though you may have your favourite genre of book, it is still a good idea to try others as variety helps you develop more reading skills.

Tip

Think about stories you know. What genre are they? Do they have a theme? What conventions do they use?

Key words

- convention
- theme

10

Challenge 1

1. Match each convention to its story genre.

a) Might use 'Once upon a time...' and, 'They lived happily ever after...'

b) The character searches for ancient hidden treasure in an unexplored jungle.

c) A time machine takes the main character to the future where she is invisible.

Adventure Story | Fairytale | Science Fiction

Read this extract from a story about a boy who sweeps chimneys and then answer the questions in Challenges 2 and 3.

Alf was woken at 6am by a loud knocking. His skinny frame was already dressed under the bed covers as the house was so cold. Racing down the stairs, he grabbed his filthy cap and went through the door onto the cobbled street. Mr Gresty was impatiently waiting with his usual mean eyes and snarling mouth. As soon as the boy appeared, Gresty walked off, leaving hungry and weak Alf to push the barrow of brushes along the street. It was still dark but they had to be early. Sweeping chimneys had to be done before the fires were lit in the grates below, not that Gresty really cared as he did not do the dirty work.

Challenge 2

1. a) What genre of fiction is this story? ______

b) Explain your answer to a). ______

Challenge 3

1. What do you know so far about the two main characters?

Total: ☐ / 7 marks

Had a go ☐ Getting there ☐ Got it! ☐

11

Five **Progress tests** included throughout the book for ongoing assessment and monitoring progress.

Mixed questions for maths and English test topics from throughout the book.

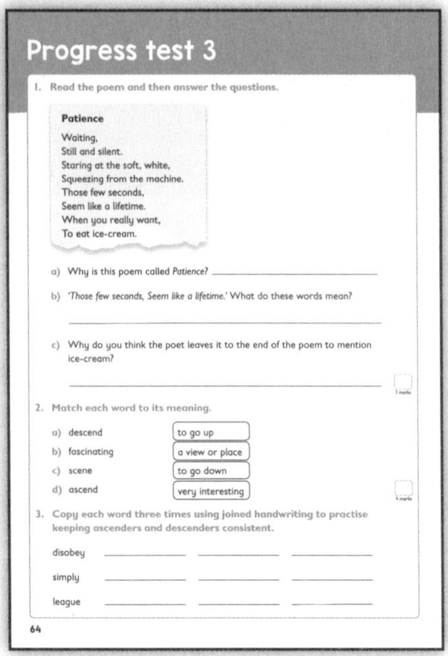

Progress test 3

1. **Read the poem and then answer the questions.**

Patience

Waiting,
Still and silent.
Staring at the soft, white,
Squeezing from the machine.
Those few seconds,
Seem like a lifetime.
When you really want,
To eat ice-cream.

a) Why is this poem called *Patience*? ______

b) '*Those few seconds, Seem like a lifetime.*' What do these words mean? ______

c) Why do you think the poet leaves it to the end of the poem to mention ice-cream? ______

2. **Match each word to its meaning.**

a) descend	to go up
b) fascinating	a view or place
c) scene	to go down
d) ascend	very interesting

3. **Copy each word three times using joined handwriting to practise keeping ascenders and descenders consistent.**

disobey ______
simply ______
league ______

64

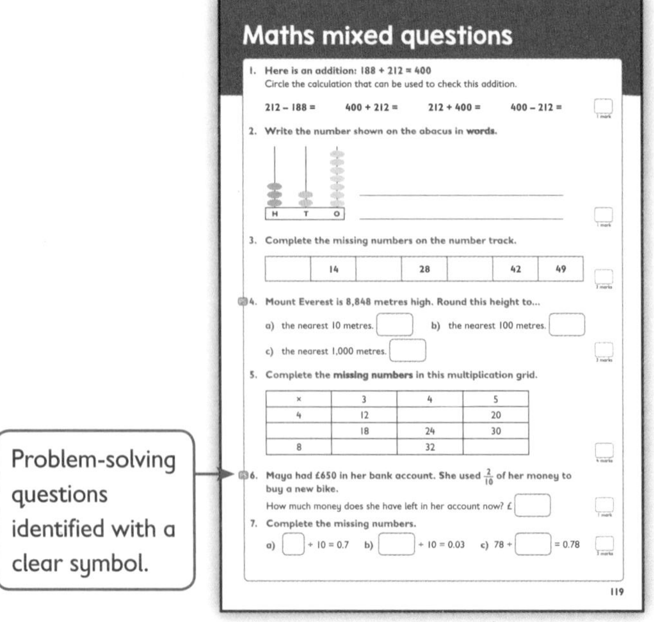

Problem-solving questions identified with a clear symbol.

Maths mixed questions

1. **Here is an addition: 188 + 212 = 400**
Circle the calculation that can be used to check this addition.
212 – 188 = 400 + 212 = 212 + 400 = 400 – 212 =

2. **Write the number shown on the abacus in words.**
H T O

3. **Complete the missing numbers on the number track.**

	14		28		42	49

4. **Mount Everest is 8,848 metres high. Round this height to...**
a) the nearest 10 metres. ☐ b) the nearest 100 metres. ☐
c) the nearest 1,000 metres. ☐

5. **Complete the missing numbers in this multiplication grid.**

×	3	4	5
4	12		20
	18	24	30
8		32	

6. **Maya had £650 in her bank account. She used $\frac{2}{10}$ of her money to buy a new bike.**
How much money does she have left in her account now? £ ☐

7. **Complete the missing numbers.**
a) ☐ ÷ 10 = 0.7 b) ☐ ÷ 10 = 0.03 c) 78 ÷ ☐ = 0.78

119

Answers provided for all the questions.

Contents

Prefixes

- Apply knowledge of prefixes to understand the meaning of words

Changing meanings of root words

The meaning of some root words can be changed by adding a **prefix**. The spelling of the root word remains the same when adding a prefix. Different prefixes have different meanings.

Examples

- not or opposite

  un- + lucky = **un**lucky — *We were unlucky in our netball match.*

  dis- + agreed = **dis**agreed — *Mason disagreed with his sister.*

  im- + mature = **im**mature — *My brother is immature.*
- again or back

  re- + appear = **re**appear — *The sun will reappear soon.*
- wrong

  mis- + understand = **mis**understand — *They need to listen in case they misunderstand anything.*

  mis- + spell = **mis**spell — *Try not to misspell any of the words.*
- under

  sub- + marine = **sub**marine — *The submarine dived beneath the sea.*
- between or among

  inter + national = **inter**national — *There was an international horse show taking place.*
- against

  anti- + social = **anti**social — *The loud music was very antisocial.*
- greater or above

  super- + market = **super**market — *The supermarket had very fresh vegetables.*
- own or self

  auto- + mobile = **auto**mobile — An automobile is a car. It means self mobile – if you have a car you can be mobile (moving) on your own.

  auto- + biography = **auto**biography — A biography is a book about someone. An autobiography is a book you write about yourself.

Remember

If you are unsure about the meaning of a word, read it in the context of the full sentence and what you already know about the text.

Tip

Make sure you know the meaning of prefixes because this will help you understand the word when reading.

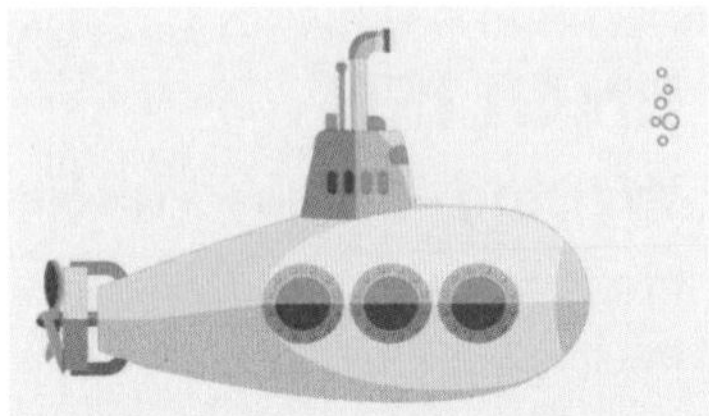

Key word

- prefix

Challenge 1

1. Add the correct prefix to each word to match the definition (meaning).

   a) Someone who saves others.

   _______hero

   b) A substance used to prevent cuts becoming septic.

   _______septic

   c) A heading which is under a main heading or title.

   _______heading

   d) To decorate something again.

   _______decorate

4 marks

Challenge 2

1. Draw a line to match each word to its definition.

a) An underground passage.	antifreeze
b) To make something new or fresh again.	subway
c) Something that is not perfect.	submarine
d) A type of ship that can go beneath the sea.	refresh
e) A substance used to prevent or stop freezing.	imperfect

5 marks

Challenge 3

1. Write the definition of each word below.

   a) submerge

   ____

   b) impatient

   ____

   c) antisocial

   ____

3 marks

Total: ☐ / 12 marks

Had a go ☐ Getting there ☐ Got it! ☐

Suffixes

- Recognise how the suffix -ation changes verbs to nouns
- Recognise the same sound written in a different way

Changing verbs to nouns

Adding the **suffix -ation** to some **verbs** changes them into a **noun**.

Example

prepare → the verb means to get ready
prepar**ation** → the noun means what you need before you do something

note – the **e** has been dropped before adding **-ation**

inform → to give information
inform**ation** → details about something

Remember

A suffix is added to a root word to change the meaning.

'shun' suffixes

Suffixes that sound like 'shun' have a number of spellings. It is important to know that these all sound the same.

Example

educate + **-tion** = educa**tion**
extend + **-sion** = exten**sion**
music + **-cian** = musi**cian**
permit + **-ssion** = permi**ssion**

Note that in each of these examples the final letter is dropped before adding the ending.

Care is needed. Some words with the **-sion** ending make a different sound – 'zhun' rather than 'shun'.

Example

- television
- decision
- invasion

Key words

- suffix
- verb
- noun

Challenge 1

1. Use the suffix **-ation** to turn each verb into a noun. Then draw a line to match each noun to its meaning.

a) relax________

b) tempt________

c) form________

d) present________

things in order

something to show

something hard to resist

rest

4 marks

Challenge 2

1. Read the list of words with the 'shun' sound at the end.
   Match each word to its meaning.

a) invention

b) exception

c) politician

d) musician

somebody who plays an instrument

something that does not follow a rule

something new

someone who speaks out about important issues

4 marks

Challenge 3

1. Add **-ation** to each verb below and use the noun this forms in the correct sentence.

imagine **admire** **expect** **prepare**

a) Sally had nearly finished the ____________________ for the party.

b) Lyall was full of ____________________ for his brave sister.

c) The ____________________ was that they would be there on time.

d) The English teacher said Jack had a great ____________________ .

4 marks

Total: ☐ / 12 marks

Had a go ☐ **Getting there** ☐ **Got it!** ☐

Word origins

- Recognise sounds in common words from different languages

Many of the words we use in English have their **word origins** in different languages. This can have an influence on the way the words sound.

ch in words of Greek origin

ch in words of Greek origin sound like the sound represented by **k** in **k**it. For example:

- s**ch**ool
- s**ch**eme

They chose a nice colour scheme.

- **ch**orus
- **ch**aracter
- **ch**emist

The chemist mixed the chemicals together.

ch in words of French origin

ch in words of French origin make a **sh** sound as represented by **sh** in **sh**op. For example:

- **ch**ef
- **ch**auffeur

This is actually a French word used in English.

The chauffeur drove the car.

- ma**ch**ine
- para**ch**ute
- bro**ch**ure

They chose a holiday from the brochure.

gue and que in words of French origin

gue at the end of a word often sounds like the sound represented by **g** in **g**ap. For example:

- collea**gue**
- va**gue**
- fati**gue**

que at the end of a word sounds like the sound represented by **k** in **k**id. For example:

- anti**que**
- uni**que**
- techni**que**

sc in words of Latin origin

The **sc** in words of Latin origin make a **s** sound as represented by **s** in **s**at. For example:

- **sc**ene
- **sc**issors
- **sc**ience
- mu**sc**les
- de**sc**end

Remember

Look out for words with different origins and notice word families that they come from.

Tip

Care is needed with spelling patterns – sometimes the same letters can make a different sound.

Key word

- word origin

Challenge 1

1. Match each statement to its word of French origin.

a) A type of conversation — antique

b) Something that isn't see-through — vague

c) Something old — dialogue

d) Not clear — opaque

4 marks

Challenge 2

1. Write each **ch** word in the correct sentence.

character **machine** **architect** **parachute**

a) They made a ________________ jump from a plane.

b) The house was designed by a brilliant ________________ .

c) Goldilocks is a fictional ________________.

d) A special ________________ is used to make paper.

4 marks

Challenge 3

1. Write a definition for each of the **sc** words below.

a) scientist

____

b) ascend

____

c) crescent

____

d) scenic

____

4 marks

Total: / 12 marks

Had a go ☐ **Getting there** ☐ **Got it!** ☐

Fiction genres

- Identify different genres
- Recognise conventions and themes

Different genres

Fiction texts come from a range of **genres** – this means the type of story.

Example

myth	fairytale	science fiction
Powerful gods and strange creatures and events.	Castles, princes, princesses and magic.	Space or futuristic with inventions that don't really exist.

Other genres include **historical fiction**, **thrillers** and **adventure stories.**

Conventions

Conventions are common features and techniques used by writers in different genres.

For example:

- A **fairytale** will often have good and evil characters and a happy ending.
- A **thriller** will have twists and turns so the reader is unsure what will happen next.
- An **adventure story** will have lots of exciting events and mishaps for the characters.

Themes in writing

Many stories have common **themes**. These are not always the subject of the writing but are ideas that the writer puts across.

Example

- friendship and relationships
- honesty
- kindness
- conflict
- good versus evil

Remember

Even though you may have your favourite genre of book, it is still a good idea to try others as variety helps you develop more reading skills.

Tip

Think about stories you know. What genre are they? Do they have a theme? What conventions do they use?

Key words

- convention
- theme

Challenge 1

1. Match each convention to its story genre.

a) Might use 'Once upon a time…' and, 'They lived happily ever after…'

b) The character searches for ancient hidden treasure in an unexplored jungle.

c) A time machine takes the main character to the future where she is invisible.

3 marks

Read this extract from a story about a boy who sweeps chimneys and then answer the questions in Challenges 2 and 3.

Alf was woken at 6am by a loud knocking. His skinny frame was already dressed under the bed covers as the house was so cold. Racing down the stairs, he grabbed his filthy cap and went through the door onto the cobbled street. Mr Gresty was impatiently waiting with his usual mean eyes and snarling mouth. As soon as the boy appeared, Gresty walked off, leaving hungry and weak Alf to push the barrow of brushes along the street. It was still dark but they had to be early. Sweeping chimneys had to be done before the fires were lit in the grates below, not that Gresty really cared as he did not do the dirty work.

Challenge 2

1. a) What genre of fiction is this story? ______________________

b) Explain your answer to a). ______________________

____

2 marks

Challenge 3

1. What do you know so far about the two main characters?

____

2 marks

____

Total: ☐ /7 marks

Had a go ☐ **Getting there** ☐ **Got it!** ☐

Poetry

- Recognise different forms of poetry
- Identify how language contributes to meaning

Poems

There are different types of **poem**, which are written in different ways.

Acrostic poems

In an **acrostic poem** the letters in the poem spell a word or phrase, often the poem title.

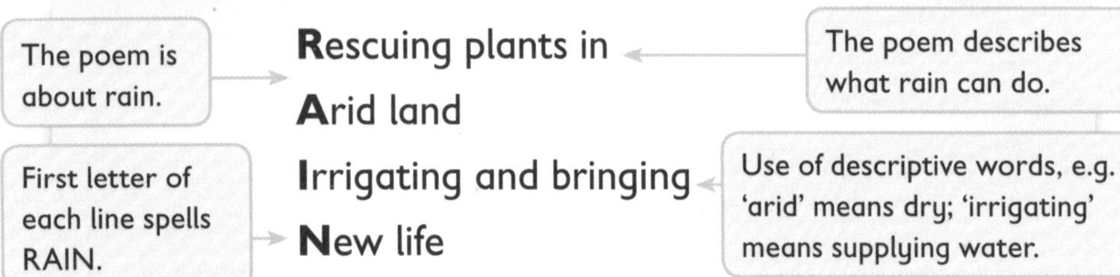

Free verse

Free verse is a poem with no set pattern or rhyme. It is often descriptive.

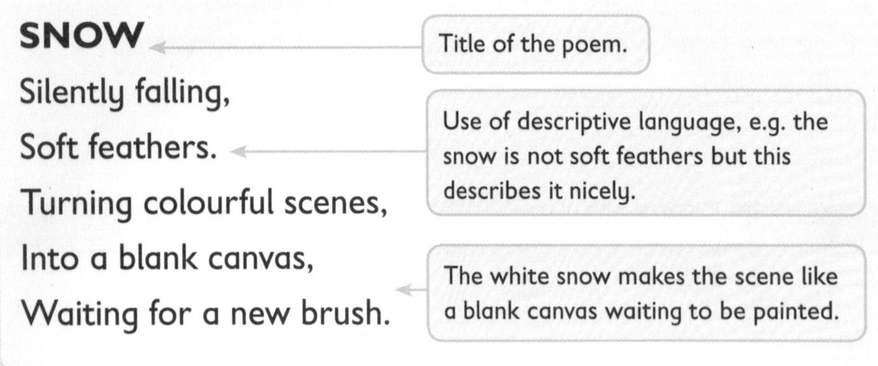

Haiku

Haiku is a type of poem that originated in Japan. Every Haiku has 17 syllables (beats): 5 syllables in the first line, 7 syllables in the second line and 5 syllables in the third line.

Winter is here
Frost arrived last night
Bitter cold sign of winter
Hats, gloves and coats on

Each line fits with the theme.

Check the number of syllables in each line.

Remember

Not all poems rhyme.

Tip

When reading and understanding poems, it is important to find out the meaning of unfamiliar words, and to work out what the poet means.

Tip

Look out for a wide variety of poems. Think about the descriptive language and the way they make you feel.

Key word

- poem

Challenge 1

1. Read the Haiku and answer the questions.

Traffic slowly crawls
Panicking we must be quick
First day at new school.

a) Write the number of syllables in each line.

Line 1: ________

Line 2: ________

Line 3: ________

b) What is causing the panic in this poem? ____________________

2 marks

Challenge 2

1. Read the poem and then answer the questions.

Cold air across my face,
Hard ground, lying still,
Eyes wide,
Staring at the heavens.

White dots,
Millions and millions,
Shapes and patterns,
Stargazing.

a) What does 'staring at the heavens' mean?

____

b) Why do you think 'hard ground' is mentioned in the second line?

____

c) What are the 'white dots' in line 5? ____________________

3 marks

Challenge 3

1. Read the acrostic poem below. Explain what the words mean in lines 2 (Relentlessly) and 4 (Impossibly fast).

The Train
Travelling
Relentlessly
Across the land
Impossibly fast
Nature blurs by

Line 2 ____________________

____

____

Line 4 ____________________

____

____

2 marks

Total: ☐ / 7 marks

Had a go ☐ **Getting there** ☐ **Got it!** ☐

Inference

- Make inferences from a text and justify these with evidence

Inferring about characters

Inference about a character's feelings, words or actions can help us understand the character and the text better.

Example

What information does the text give about Lola?

> Katy was very chatty. In fact she did not really stop talking. There was lots of information about herself. Lola rolled her eyes as Katy started yet another sentence. Jack and Priya sat listening politely. Katy was the new girl in the class and seemed nice enough.
>
> "Come on you two," interrupted Lola. "Let's go and do something else," she said, walking away and signalling for Jack and Priya to follow.

Jack and Priya listened politely – this contrasts with Lola rolling her eyes and then walking away.

Lola only asks Jack and Priya to go with her, not Katy. She leaves Katy out.

At first it looks like the text does not give any information about Lola other than her name.
However, it can be inferred that Lola is being unkind to Katy – rolling her eyes shows she feels bored of her, and walking away and not including Katy shows that Lola is being mean.

Tip

Read between the lines. This means that you should think what the words are really saying.

Inferring from a non-fiction text

Sometimes inferences can be made from a non-fiction text, particularly about the author's point of view.

Key word

- inference

Example

> A new airport would be a boost for local business. Lots more people would be coming to the area and more hotels would be needed. However, farmland would be lost to build the airport. There would also be lots of noise and pollution, which would stop people visiting. None of the hotels would be owned by local people. And who would want a noisy, dirty airport on their doorstep?

Gives both sides of the argument, but the question at the end and the words 'noisy, dirty' suggest the author's point of view.

It appears at first that the author is giving a balanced argument about the airport but with a little inference it can be seen that the author has their own point of view.

Challenge 1

1. Read the text below.

Cars are great for travel. They are very convenient. Most families have a car and they use them daily. They are also bad for the environment and are destroying our planet.

Find and copy two words that help us to infer that the author has a negative view of cars.

____

____

2 marks

Challenge 2

1. Read the text below.

The teacher glared at Daisy. Her lip trembled and she wanted to explain that she had not made the silly noise, but she knew there was no point. Louis turned away, grinning. He had got away with it.

a) What do the words 'lip trembled' suggest about how Daisy was feeling?

____

b) Explain what can be inferred about Louis from the text.

____

2 marks

Challenge 3

1. Write a sentence for each of the words in bold below that imply how the character is feeling without actually using the word.

a) Cam is **happy**.

____

b) Anil is **sad**.

____

2 marks

Total: ☐ /6 marks

Had a go ☐ Getting there ☐ Got it! ☐

Performance and understanding

- Show understanding through intonation, tone and volume when reading aloud

Reading aloud

Thinking about how words, phrases and sentences should be read aloud helps with the understanding of a text. **Intonation** is how things are said and it gives clues about feelings and ideas.

The words below, particularly the spoken words, "When will we get there?" could be read in different ways:

> "When will we get there?" asked Cory. The journey had been long and she wanted to get out of the car.

Reading them in an **excited** voice would make Cory sound excited. Reading them in a **bored** voice would show that Cory is actually bored.

The words below are describing a creepy scene in a story:

> Little light came through the windows. Dusty cobwebs hung from the old, musty furniture. The small boy shivered a little, although it was not cold. As he did so, the door handle started to turn. Who, or what, could it be?

The words should be read slowly and quietly to build up some tension. Reading them too quickly or loudly would spoil the spooky atmosphere that the words create.

Remember

Look for clues in the text about how characters are feeling. Think about what they say and what they do.

Playscripts

Playscripts give clues about how characters speak or behave. These clues help when reading a playscript and bring the action to life when performing.

Girl *(pleading)*:	Please help us. We need shelter.
Gentleman *(shocked)*:	Oh my! You poor things.
Girl *(sobbing)*:	We lost our way in the snowstorm.
Gentleman *(urgently)*:	Come in, come in. Get out of this cold.

The way the words are spoken are written in brackets. This helps when getting into a role as a character. If the words were said in a different way, they would not mean the same thing.

Tip

In a script, directions (given in italics, brackets or both) provide help about the way the script should be read.

Key word

- intonation

Challenge 1

1. Match each sentence to the adverb that best describes how it should be read.

a)	b)	c)
"Get out! Now!" screamed Mummy Bear at Goldilocks.	"Somebody has eaten all my porridge," wept Baby Bear.	"My poor baby bear," whispered Daddy Bear.

sadly **quietly** **angrily**

3 marks

Challenge 2

1. Read the playscript text below and add a word in each space to describe how the character is speaking.

   a) Jack (____________________): Look, look Mum! I've got some amazing magic beans.

   b) Mum (____________________): What! You mean to say you sold our cow for magic beans? You fool!

   c) Jack (____________________): I'm sorry Mum. I'm sorry.

3 marks

Challenge 3

1. Read the text below. Explain how you think it should be read.

> Tumbling, spinning, rolling, bouncing. Faster and faster. The children giggled as the huge ball made its own way down the steep slope. Then it stopped. There was silence. The ball was still and the glass door it had rolled into had a large crack.

____

____

2 marks

Total: ☐ /8 marks

Had a go ☐ **Getting there** ☐ **Got it!** ☐

Non-fiction conventions

- **Identify features and conventions in non-fiction texts**

Features

Non-fiction texts generally have similar **text features**.

For example:

- contents page
- interesting and relevant facts
- subheadings
- illustrations – photographs and diagrams
- glossary
- index

Conventions

There are general **conventions** (common features and techniques) in non-fiction writing.

Example

Healthy Eating

Eating healthy food helps the body grow and develop as it should. It also plays a role in preventing and overcoming illness.

A balanced diet

Choosing food from a range of food groups provides everything the body needs. Calcium from dairy products, proteins from meat, and vitamins from fruit and vegetables can all form part of a balanced diet.

Unhealthy food

While unhealthy food such as sugars and fats can be enjoyable, they should be avoided in large quantities.

The text is **impersonal** so it does not refer to 'you' or 'I'. It is written in the third person and uses names of objects or the theme. Some texts will be about a person and they will use the person's name and he/she/they.

Formal language is used, e.g. vocabulary such as 'preventing' rather than 'stopping' and 'overcoming' rather than 'getting better'.

Technical words are used, e.g. calcium, protein, vitamin.

When reading a non-fiction text, it is important to gain an understanding of what some of the words and ideas mean. Use the **glossary** and a **dictionary** to help with this.

Key words

- text feature
- convention
- glossary
- dictionary

Read the non-fiction text below and answer the questions in Challenges 1 to 3.

The Water Cycle

The processes of evaporation and condensation play an important role in the Earth's weather patterns and in the water cycle that is so important for life on Earth.

Evaporation

As the sun heats the surface of bodies of water (oceans, lakes and rivers), the water from the surface becomes a gas (water vapour) and rises into the sky.

Condensation

As the water vapour rises, it starts to cool down and condense, forming clouds. Clouds consist of millions of droplets of water.

Challenge 1

1. Match the convention to the correct example from the text.

   a) 'it starts to cool down and condense'

   b) 'evaporation and condensation'

   c) 'forming clouds'

   technical words

   formal language

   third person writing

   3 marks

Challenge 2

1. a) The text uses the words, 'Clouds consist of… '. What does **consist** mean?

   ____

   b) It also says, 'the sun heats the surface of bodies of water'. What does **bodies of water** mean?

   ____

   2 marks

Challenge 3

1. a) What causes the surface of the water to become water vapour?

   ____

   b) Why does the water vapour condense?

   ____

   ____

   2 marks

Total: ☐ /7 marks

Had a go ☐ **Getting there** ☐ **Got it!** ☐

Using information from texts

- Identify the main ideas and summarise information from a text

Summarising information

Summarising a text means selecting the main information and details before putting them into your own words.

For example, on the right is a summary of the story of *Goldilocks and the Three Bears*.

The Bear family went out. A girl called Goldilocks entered their home. She tried their porridge, sat on their chairs (breaking Baby Bear's chair) and lay on their beds. She fell asleep on Baby Bear's bed. The Bears returned home. They found Goldilocks and chased her away.

Using information

Rather than just summarising information, sometimes there is a need to use the information. Questions might need answering about the text, or ideas from the text may be needed to help write another text. **Evidence** is found for key ideas.

Tip

Look for examples in the text as evidence for key points.

Example

What positives and negatives are there about this restaurant?

positive – luxurious; **evidence** – fine art, carpet and comfortable chairs

negative – expensive

The restaurant is excellent but rather expensive. Our table had to be reserved several weeks in advance as it is so popular.

positive – popular

From the outside it looks quite plain but inside the decoration is luxurious. Fine art hangs from the walls, the red carpet is thick and soft, and the chairs are a pleasure to sit upon. It is a shame that there are too many tables. Everybody seems very close and conversations can easily be overheard.

negative – too many tables; **evidence** – people too close together

However, the food is delightful. From the starter to the dessert, everything was of the highest quality. Exceptional and delicate flavours made it a meal to remember.

positive – high quality food; **evidence** – exceptional and delicate flavours

The fine but cramped dining was only made more magnificent by the wonderful staff for whom nothing was too much trouble.

positive – wonderful staff; **evidence** – nothing too much trouble

Key words

- summary
- evidence

Challenge 1

1. Write a brief summary of a well-known story.

____

____

____

3 marks

Read this text and then answer the questions in Challenges 2 and 3.

There is much debate about the building of the new road. It will bring jobs to the area and reduce journey times. However, there are concerns about the environment.

The journey between East Braxton and West Upham will be cut by 20 minutes. It will remove half of the traffic from the busy Greenway junction, which not only sees regular jams but also several accidents per year. The local council has stated that a new road would be of great benefit to each town.

Environmental groups argue that there will be too much damage. The road will pass through Old Nook – an ancient woodland which is home to rare bats and a wide variety of plants. Once this has gone it will never return. They believe that there will also be more cars.

Challenge 2

1. Write two key **facts** from the text.

____

____

2 marks

Challenge 3

1. a) Some people think the new road will damage the environment.

   What evidence is there in the text for this opinion?

   ____

   b) Give one argument from the text for the new road being a good idea.

   ____

2 marks

Total: ☐ / 7 marks

Had a go ☐ **Getting there** ☐ **Got it!** ☐

Progress test I

1. **Add the correct prefix to each word.**

a) a medicine: ________biotic

b) large shop: ________market

c) between countries: ________national

d) appear again: ________appear

e) go under water: ________merge

5 marks

2. **Change each of these verbs into a noun by adding the suffix -ation.**

a) admire ____________________

b) invite ____________________

c) inform ____________________

d) prepare ____________________

e) transport ____________________

5 marks

3. **Write each gue word in the correct sentence.**

vague **fatigue** **colleague** **intrigue** **meringue**

a) There was lots of ______________ about the new teacher.

b) We ate a delicious ______________ for dessert.

c) The reason for the cancelled show was quite ______________.

d) ______________ finally made Tom sit and rest.

e) At Mum's work we met her ______________, Janet.

5 marks

4. **Write a definition for each of the ch words below.**

a) anchor

____

b) architect

____

c) moustache

____

d) brochure

____

e) machine

____

f) chorus

____

6 marks

5. **Read this extract about a girl who travels into space.**

Even if told something was too hard, Milly had never given up.

"You won't be able to go into space, Milly," they'd warned. "You're too small."

Now, she faced a huge problem. She knew this was the hardest thing she had ever attempted but she also knew that if she failed she would never see home again.

Her spaceship needed to land. Urgent work was needed on the engine but to fix it she had to stop. Milly had guided the craft to the surface of a small planet. Almost. As she flew low over purple rocks and orange trees she could see gaps in which she could land. She could also see that these gaps were very small. One mistake and her spaceship would be damaged beyond repair.

a) What genre of fiction is this story?

____

b) Explain your answer to part a).

c) What can we infer about Milly from the first two lines of text?

3 marks

6. **Read the Haiku poem below then answer the questions.**

Painstaking movement
Slow, steady, calm but onwards
To meet other slugs.

a) What does **painstaking movement** mean?

b) What is the poem about?

c) Explain the main feature of a Haiku poem.

3 marks

7. **Write a sentence for each word in bold below that shows how the character is feeling without actually using the word.**

a) Jess is **hungry**.

b) Eli is **excited**.

2 marks

8. Read the playscript below and add a word in each space to describe how the character is speaking.

a) Mum (__________________): Zoe, please set the table darling.

b) Zoe: (__________________): No! It's not fair! I always have to set the table!

c) Mum: (__________________): Then go to your room young lady.

3 marks

9. Read the text.

The votes are open for the best seaside resort in England. Will the winner be brilliant Blackpool or will it be Scarborough?

Both are fantastic places. Scarborough has lovely beaches. Blackpool's beaches are big and spacious. Both have got lots of hotels and car parks and Blackpool has a motorway nearby, making it really easy to get to.

Whichever wins, it is sure to be a close vote.

a) Find and copy two words or phrases that infer that the author likes Blackpool more than Scarborough.

____

____

2 marks

b) Tick the pair of subheadings that would fit best for the next sections of the given text.

i) What people like about the seaside
Why people go to the seaside ☐

ii) Booming Blackpool
Super Scarborough ☐

iii) Lots to do at both places
Why I like Blackpool best ☐

1 mark

Total: ☐ /35 marks

Reading and writing 4-digit whole numbers

- Understand the place value of each digit in a 4-digit number
- Show how numbers can be represented in different ways
- Read Roman numerals up to 100 (I to C)

Place value

The value of each digit in a number depends on its position or place in the number. This is called the **place value** of a digit.

Example

Let's look at the number 6,666.

Each digit is the same **but** the value of each digit is different.

To work out the value of each digit, it is helpful to label the number.

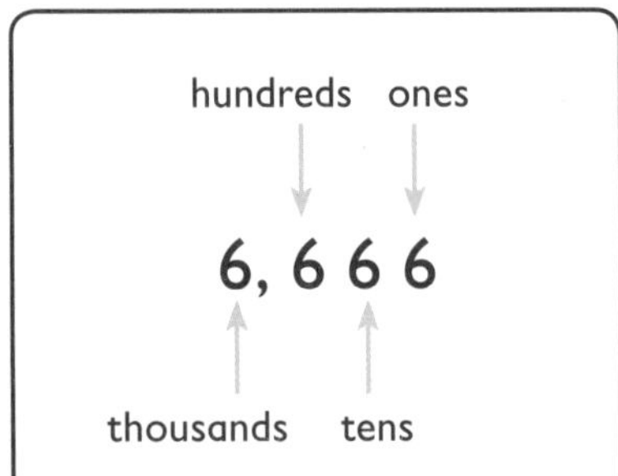

We can see this number is made up of 6,000 (6 **thousands**) + 600 (6 **hundreds**) + 60 (6 **tens**) + 6 (6 **ones**)

This number can be shown in different ways:

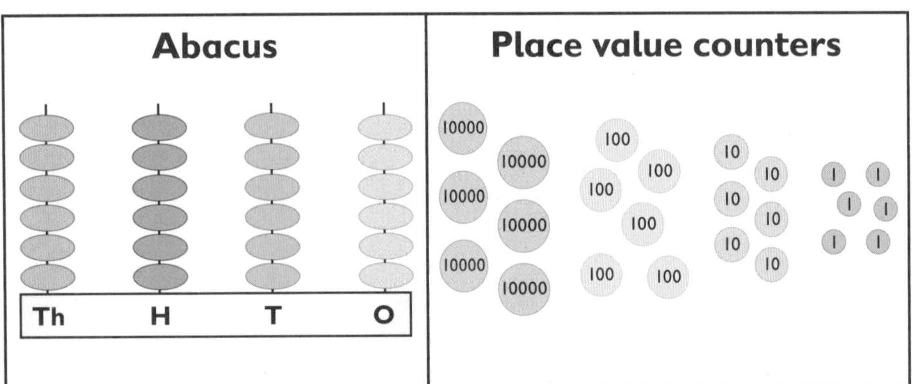

Knowing the value of each digit helps us write the number in words or numerals:

Six thousand, six hundred and sixty-six ← words

6,666 ← numerals

Roman numerals

Roman numerals are the numbers that were used in the time of ancient Rome. The numerals use letters or combinations of letters from the Latin alphabet, e.g. I, V, X, L and C.

Roman numerals				
I	V	X	L	C
1	5	10	50	100

Key words

- place value
- thousand
- hundred
- ten
- one
- Roman numeral

Challenge 1

1. Write the value of the **hundreds** digit in each of these numbers.

a) 317 ______ b) 570 ______ c) 929______ d) 791 ______

4 marks

2. Write the value of the **thousands** digit in each of these numbers.

a) 2,179 ______ b) 4,200 ______ c) 6,543 ______ d) 8,152 ______

4 marks

3. Write these numbers in Roman numerals.

a) 5 ______ b) 50 ______ c) 35 ______ d) 19 ______

4 marks

Challenge 2

1. Complete the table to show each number on an abacus, in numerals and in words.

Abacus	Th H T O	Th H T O	Th H T O
Number in numerals		6,505	
Number in words			Nine thousand, three hundred and ninety

6 marks

Challenge 3

1. Write the Roman numerals in numbers.

a) LXV ☐ b) IX ☐ c) C ☐

3 marks

PS 2. Th H T O

Meg says, 'This shows three thousand, three hundred and sixteen ones'.

Jack says, 'This shows three thousand, three hundred, one ten and six ones'.

Who is correct? Meg ☐ Jack ☐ Both ☐

Explain your answer. ______________________________

____

1 mark

Total: ☐ / 22 marks

Had a go ☐ **Getting there** ☐ **Got it!** ☐

Comparing and ordering 4-digit whole numbers

- Understand the place value of each digit in a 4-digit number
- Order and compare numbers beyond 1,000
- Round any number to the nearest 10, 100 and 1,000

Ordering

When you put numbers in **order**, you need to think about how the numbers compare with each other.

When comparing numbers you will use:

- **place value** to help you
- words such as **bigger**, **biggest**, **larger**, **largest**, **smaller**, **smallest**, **highest**, **lowest**
- the symbols **<**, **>** and **=**.

> means '**greater than**'
< means '**less than**'
= means '**equal to**'

Example

Look at this pair of numbers. Which is larger?

8,580 **8,956**

First, look at the value of the **digit** in the **thousands** column. The value of the thousands digit is the same in both the numbers. So, you need to move on and look at the value of the hundreds digit.

8,956 is **larger than** 8,580 because it has 9 hundreds (900), which is greater than 5 hundreds (500).

8,956 **>** **8,580**

Rounding

Rounding is a way of changing a number to the nearest 10, 100 or 1,000. You will either **round up** or **round down**.

Example

Round 3,527 to the nearest...

- 10
- 100
- 1,000

To round to the nearest 10, look at the value of the ones digit. It is more than 5 ones, so you round up: 3,527 to 3,530

To round to the nearest 100, look at the value of the tens digit. It is less than 5 tens, so you round down: 3,527 to 3,500

To round to the nearest 1,000, look at the value of the hundreds digit. It has 5 hundreds, so you round up: 3,527 to 4,000

Tip

Round up if the value of the digit is 5 or more. Round down if the value of the digit is 4 or less.

Key words

- order
- greater than
- less than
- equal to
- digit
- rounding
- round up
- round down

Challenge 1

1. Write these numbers in order of size, starting with the smallest.

a) 5,708 4,910 5,555 4,870 ______ ______ ______ ______

b) 6,179 6,862 6,061 6,990 ______ ______ ______ ______

2 marks

2. Round these numbers to the nearest 10.

a) 54 ______ b) 69 ______ c) 85 ______

3 marks

3. Round these numbers to the nearest 100.

a) 142 ______ b) 459 ______ c) 304 ______

3 marks

4. Round these numbers to the nearest 1,000.

a) 1,425 ______ b) 3,795 ______ c) 2,500 ______

3 marks

Challenge 2

PS 1. Work out the missing digit.

a) 5,224 > 5☐16 b) ☐586 < 5,785

2 marks

2. Complete the table.

Number	Rounded to the nearest 10	Rounded to the nearest 100	Rounded to the nearest 1,000
4,567		4,600	
3,291	3,290		

4 marks

Challenge 3

PS 1. Here are 4 digit cards. 1 9 4 3

Use the digit cards to write:

a) the largest possible number ______

b) the smallest possible number ______

c) a number that when rounded to the nearest thousand is 2,000

______

3 marks

Total: ☐ / 20 marks

Had a go ☐ Getting there ☐ Got it! ☐

Negative numbers and finding 1,000 more or less

- Count backwards through zero to include negative numbers
- Find 1,000 more or less than a given number

Negative numbers

Numbers do not just stop at **zero**. When you count **backwards** from **zero**, you go into **negative numbers.**

- Positive numbers are more than zero, e.g. 1, 2, 3, 4, 5, etc.
- Negative numbers are less than zero, e.g. −1, −2, −3, −4, −5, etc.
- Zero, 0, is neither positive nor negative.

A **number line** can be used to order negative and positive numbers.

Here is an example of a number line:

1,000 more or less

To find 1,000 **more** or 1,000 **less** than a number you need to **add** or **subtract** one thousand in the **thousands column**.

Example

Laura has 5,642 beads.

Th H T O

She **adds 1,000 more**.

She now has 6,642 beads.

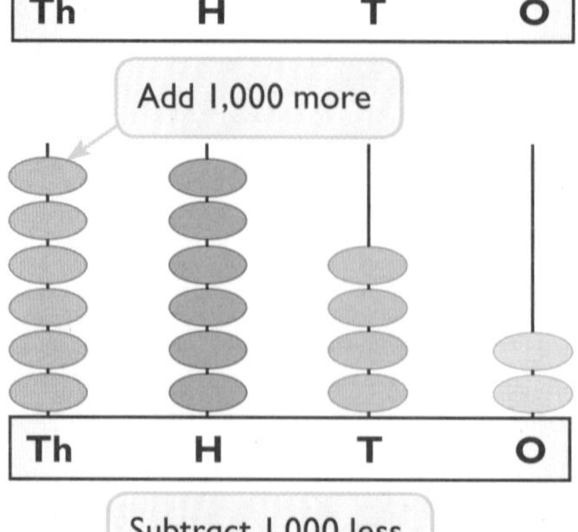

She **subtracts 1,000 less**.

She now has 4,642 beads.

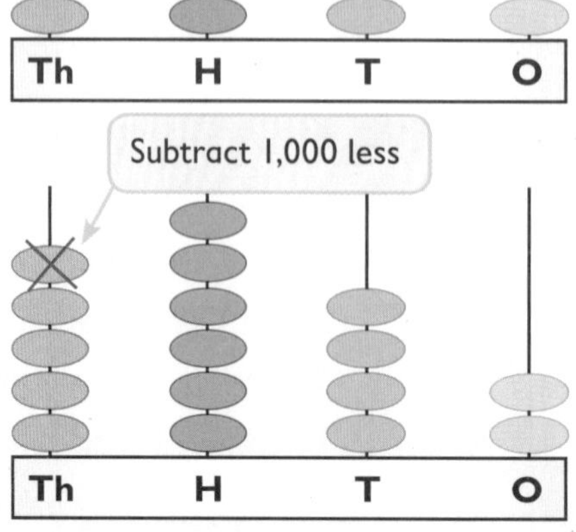

Key words

- more
- less
- addition
- subtraction

Challenge 1

1. Find **1,000 more** than each number.

   a) 6,766 ________ b) 9,070 ________ c) 1,250 ________ d) 2,950 ________ 4 marks

2. Find **1,000 less** than each number.

   a) 3,565 ________ b) 7,650 ________ c) 5,642 ________ d) 9,121 ________ 4 marks

Challenge 2

1. Complete the table.

1,000 more	Start number	1,000 less
	7,894	
4,539		
		345

6 marks

PS 2. Here is a thermometer scale.

°C

–8 –7 –6 –4 –3 –2 –1 0 1 2 3 4 5

   a) Write the temperature that is missing from the thermometer. ________ °C

   b) If the temperature on the thermometer is –2°C and it rises by 3 degrees, what is the new temperature? ________ °C

2 marks

Challenge 3

PS 1. Here are four money boxes:

A: £3,564 **B:** £2,666 **C:** £4,666 **D:** £3,864

Mai adds £100 to money box A and adds £1,000 to money box B. She takes £1,000 from money box C and takes £100 from money box D. Tick the money boxes that have the same amount of money after Mai has exchanged the money.

A ☐ **B** ☐ **C** ☐ **D** ☐

1 mark

PS 2. A fridge has 3 levels. The top level is at 5°C, but the lowest level is 7 degrees cooler. Ted says, 'The lowest level is at 12°C'. Do you agree? Explain your answer.

____

____

1 mark

Total: ☐ **/ 18 marks**

Had a go ☐ **Getting there** ☐ **Got it!** ☐

Counting in multiples

- Count in multiples of 6, 7, 9, 25 and 1,000

Multiples

6 × 7 grid

Multiplying is the same as using the word **times**.

- For example, '6 times 7' is the same as '6 multiplied by 7 (6 × 7)'.

You can also think of multiplying as repeated addition.

So, 6 × 7 is the same as 6 + 6 + 6 + 6 + 6 + 6 + 6.

The result of multiplying one number by another is a **multiple**.

- For example, **42** is a multiple of 6 because 6 × 7 = 42.

The difference between each multiple is always the same.

- For example: **0** (add 6) **6** (add 6) **12** (add 6) **18** (add 6) **24** (add 6) **30** …

Multiples of 6, 7 and 9

Here are some of the multiples of 6:	Here are some of the multiples of 7:	Here are some of the multiples of 9:
6 × 1 = 6	7 × 1 = 7	9 × 1 = 9
6 × 2 = 12	7 × 2 = 14	9 × 2 = 18
6 × 3 = 18	7 × 3 = 21	9 × 3 = 27
6 × 4 = 24	7 × 4 = 28	9 × 4 = 36
6 × 5 = 30	7 × 5 = 35	9 × 5 = 45
6 × 6 = 36…	7 × 6 = 42…	9 × 6 = 54…
… 42, 48, 54, 60, 66, 72…	… 49, 56, 63, 70, 77, 84…	… 63, 72, 81, 90, 99, 108…

Multiples of 25 and 1,000

Multiples of 25:	0	25	50	75	100	125...

Multiples of 1,000:	0	1,000	2,000	3,000	4,000...

Key word

- multiple

Challenge 1

1. Complete the missing numbers in each number track.

a)	**0**	**1,000**		**3,000**	**4,000**	
b)	**0**	**25**		**75**	**100**	
c)	**0**	**6**	**12**	**18**		
d)	**0**	**9**		**27**		**45**

8 marks

Challenge 2

1. Circle the odd one out in each number sequence.

a) 25 50 75 100 125 160 200 225

b) 0 6 12 16 18 24 30 36

c) 9 18 27 32 45 54 63 72

3 marks

2. Look at each number string. Which multiples do they show?

a) 42, 36, 30, 24, 18 Multiples of ________

b) 4,000, 5,000, 6,000, 7,000, 8,000 Multiples of ________

c) 56, 49, 42, 35, 28 Multiples of ________

d) 200, 175, 150, 125, 100 Multiples of ________

4 marks

Challenge 3

PS 1. For each statement, choose either true or false and explain your reason.

a) Multiples of 25 always end in the digit 5. True ☐ False ☐

Reason: ________________________________

b) Multiples of 1,000 always end in the digit 0. True ☐ False ☐

Reason: ________________________________

c) Multiples of 7 are always odd numbers. True ☐ False ☐

Reason: ________________________________

d) Multiples of 9 are always less than 100. True ☐ False ☐

Reason: ________________________________

8 marks

Total: ☐ /23 marks

Had a go ☐ **Getting there** ☐ **Got it!** ☐

Adding in columns

- Use a column method to add numbers with up to four digits
- Estimate the answer to a calculation and use the inverse operation to check the answer
- Solve complex addition problems including missing number problems

The symbol for **addition** is +. There are many different words that can be used for addition.

Addition words

- sum
- add
- plus
- total
- altogether
- more than
- increase

Adding mentally

Numbers can be added in your head (the mental method) using place value and number bonds to help.

Example

Calculate 2,700 + 1,200 using a **mental method**.

You can partition the numbers into thousands, hundreds, tens and ones to help:

2,000 + 1,000 = 3,000; 700 + 200 = 900.

So, 3,000 + 900 = 3,900

Written method

When calculating numbers using a written method we can:

1. **Estimate** 2. **Calculate** 3. **Check**

Example

Calculate 4,528 + 1,034 using a formal written method.

Estimate: Round each number to the nearest thousand, so 5,000 + 1,000 = 6,000

Calculate: You can set out the calculation like this:

	Th	H	T	O
	4	5	2	8
+	1	0	3	4
	5	5	6	2
			1	

Step 1: Add the ones: 8 + 4 = 12 which is 1 ten and 2 ones. Write the 2 ones in the ones **column** but **carry** the 1 ten to the tens column and write it under the line.

Step 2: Add the tens: 20 + 30 = 50. But don't forget to add the carried 1 ten so 20 + 30 + 10 = 60

Step 3: Add the hundreds: 500 + 0 = 500. Write 500 in the hundreds column. (But remember if you had more than 10 hundreds then you would need to carry to the thousands column.)

Step 4: Add the thousands: 4,000 + 1,000 = 5,000

Check: You can check your answer using the **inverse** (opposite) operation. The inverse operation of addition is subtraction, so 5,562 – 1,034 = 4,528.

Tip

Make sure you place each digit in the correct place value column when adding in columns.

Key words

- addition
- estimate
- calculate
- check
- column
- carry
- inverse

Challenge 1

1. Calculate using a mental method.

a) 200 + 900 = ______

b) 640 + 820 = ______

c) 760 + 550 = ______

d) 1,000 + 3,200 = ______

e) 5,600 + 2,200 = ______

f) 4,010 + 3,080 = ______

g) 6,300 + 7,405 = ______

h) 1,290 + 1,320 = ______

8 marks

Challenge 2

1. Complete the calculations.

a)

	Th	H	T	O
	4	7	5	7
+			4	8

Estimate ______
Answer ______
Check ______

b)

	Th	H	T	O
	5	2	7	7
+		2	8	6

Estimate ______
Answer ______
Check ______

c)

	Th	H	T	O
	6	2	6	2
+	3	4	2	8

Estimate ______
Answer ______
Check ______

d)

	Th	H	T	O
	2	2	7	7
+	1	7	7	5

Estimate ______
Answer ______
Check ______

4 marks

Challenge 3

PS 1. Solve these word problems.

a) At a football match there are 5,515 West Field fans and 3,525 Liverside fans.

What is the total number of fans in the stadium? ______

b) In the library, there are 3,785 science books in one bookcase and 4,555 science books in another bookcase. How many science books are there altogether? ______

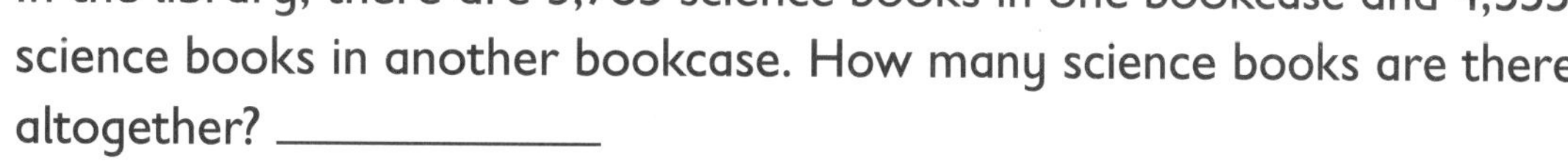

2 marks

PS 2. Complete the missing numbers on the number pyramid.

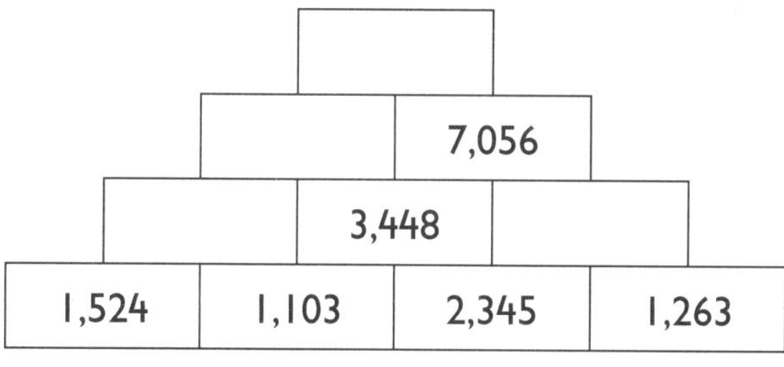

4 marks

Total: /18 marks

Had a go ☐ Getting there ☐ Got it! ☐

Subtracting in columns

- Use a column method to subtract numbers with up to four digits
- Estimate the answer to a calculation and use the inverse operation to check the answer
- Solve complex subtraction problems including missing number problems

The symbol for **subtraction** is –. There are many different words that can be used for **subtraction**.

Subtraction words
- take away
- less than
- minus
- decrease
- difference
- fewer

Subtracting mentally

Numbers can be subtracted in your head (the mental method) using place value and number bonds to help.

Example

Calculate 5,700 – 1,200 using a **mental method**.

You can partition the number into thousands, hundreds, tens and ones to help:

5,000 – 1,000 = 4,000; 700 – 200 = 500

So, 4,000 + 500 = 4,500

Written method

When calculating numbers using a written method we can:

1. **Estimate** 2. **Calculate** 3. **Check**

Example

Calculate 5,275 – 2,954 using a formal written method.

Estimate: Round each number to the nearest thousand:
5,000 – 3,000 = 2,000

Calculate: You can set out the calculation like this:

	Th	H	T	O
	⁴~~5~~	¹2	7	5
–	2	9	5	4
	2	3	2	1

Step 1: Subtract the ones: 5 – 4 = 1. Write the 1 in the ones **column**.
Step 2: Subtract the tens: 70 – 50 = 20. Write 20 in the tens column.
Step 3: Subtract the hundreds: 200 – 900. But, because you can't take 900 from 200, you need to **exchange** 5 thousands for 4 thousands and 1 thousand, and add the 1 thousand to the hundreds column. So, 1200 – 900 = 300. Write 300 in the hundreds column.
Step 4: Subtract the thousands: 4,000 – 2,000 = 2,000. Write 2,000 in the thousands column.

Check: You can check your answer using the **inverse** (opposite) operation. The inverse operation of subtraction is addition. So, 2,321 + 2,954 = 5,275

Tip

Make sure you place each digit in the correct place value column when subtracting in columns.

Key words

- subtraction
- estimate
- calculate
- check
- column
- exchange
- inverse

Challenge 1

1. Calculate using a mental method.

a) 2,300 – 1,200 = ________

b) 4,200 – 1,120 = ________

c) 4,680 – 2,400 = ________

d) 3,500 – 1,600 = ________

e) 8,580 – 1,640 = ________

f) 7,350 – 2,530 = ________

g) 8,740 – 3,350 = ________

h) 9,200 – 3,400 = ________

8 marks

Challenge 2

1. a)

	Th	H	T	O
	1	6	9	5
–		2	4	3

Estimate ________
Answer ________
Check ________

b)

	Th	H	T	O
	7	2	0	6
–		8	1	9

Estimate ________
Answer ________
Check ________

c)

	Th	H	T	O
	7	0	7	0
–	5	2	5	4

Estimate ________
Answer ________
Check ________

d)

	Th	H	T	O
	2	1	6	8
–	1	0	2	2

Estimate ________
Answer ________
Check ________

4 marks

Challenge 3

PS 1. Solve these word problems.

a) Ren is playing a video game. She started with 5,250 gold coins but has lost 1,342 gold coins.

How many gold coins does she have left?

____

b) There are 1,099 sheets of paper in a box. Tammy uses 367 sheets of paper for printing.

How many sheets of paper are left in the box?

____

2 marks

Total: ☐ / 14 marks

Had a go ☐ **Getting there** ☐ **Got it!** ☐

Mental methods for multiplication and division

- Recall multiplication and division facts for multiplication tables up to 12 × 12
- Recognise and use factor pairs
- Use place value and known facts to multiply and divide mentally (including multiplying by 0 and 1, and dividing by 1)
- Multiply together three numbers

Multiplication and division facts

Example

This array shows the **multiplication** fact: 3 × 4 or 4 × 3
If we count the **total** number of stars, we know that 3 × 4 = 12. We know that:
- 12 is the **product** of 3 × 4 and 4 × 3
- 3 and 4 are one of the **factor pairs** of 12

Tip

A number can have more than one factor pair, e.g. 12 has three factor pairs: 1 × 12, 3 × 4 and 6 × 2

You can use your times table facts to find **division** facts.

Example

If 4 × 3 = 12 and 3 × 4 = 12, then:

- 12 ÷ 3 = 4

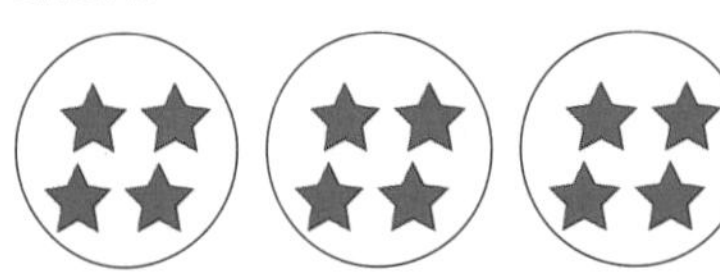

or

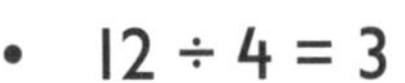

- 12 ÷ 4 = 3

Once you know that 3 × 4 = 12 or 4 × 3 = 12 and 12 ÷ 3 = 4 or 12 ÷ 4 = 3, then you can use place value to find many more facts, such as:

30 × 4 = 120 40 × 3 = 120 300 × 4 = 1,200 400 × 3 = 1,200

120 ÷ 3 = 40 120 ÷ 4 = 30 1,200 ÷ 3 = 400 1,200 ÷ 4 = 300

Multiplying three numbers

When multiplying three numbers together, first multiply the first two numbers together and then multiply the answer by the third number.

Example

Calculate 3 × 4 × 6

You need to multiply the first two numbers: 3 × 4 = 12

Then you need to multiply 12 by 6: 12 × 6 = 72

So, 3 × 4 × 6 = 72

Key words

- multiplication
- product
- factor pair
- division

Challenge 1

1. Complete the multiplication grids.

a)

×	4
4	
7	
9	
12	

b)

×	6
3	
6	
8	
9	

c)

×	8
5	
9	
6	
7	

d)

×	5
5	
6	
12	
7	

e)

×	7
7	
9	
4	
3	

20 marks

2. Circle the **factor pair** for each product.

a) 15 **2 × 3** **3 × 5** **3 × 9**

b) 21 **4 × 4** **1 × 9** **7 × 3**

2 marks

Challenge 2

1. Complete the division calculations.

a) 21 ÷ 3 = ☐ b) 36 ÷ 3 = ☐ c) 18 ÷ 3 = ☐

d) 64 ÷ 8 = ☐ e) 56 ÷ 7 = ☐ f) 96 ÷ 8 = ☐

6 marks

2. These are multiplication triangles. Multiply all three numbers around the triangle and write the answer in the middle of the triangle.

a)
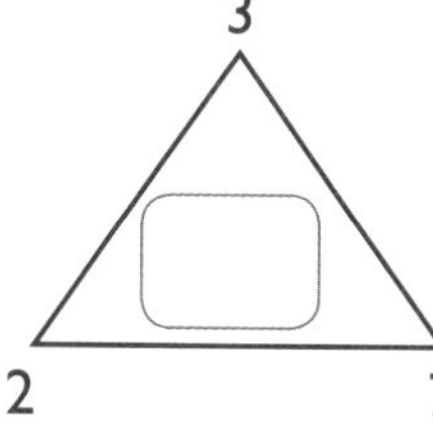

b)
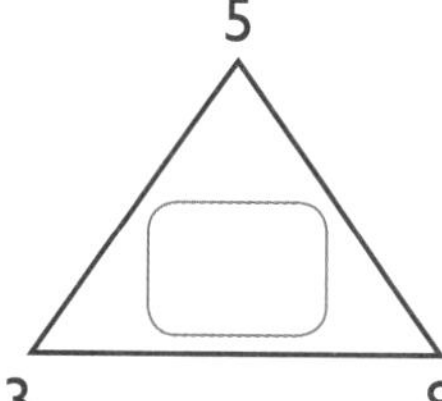

c)
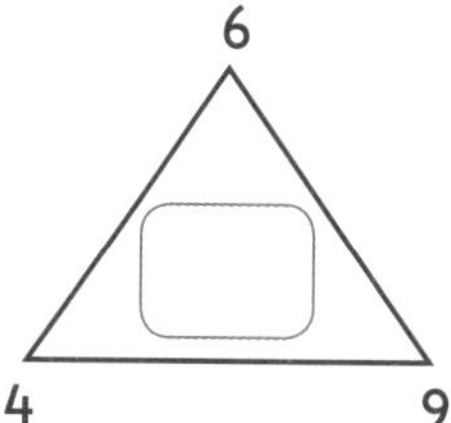

3 marks

Challenge 3

PS 1. Write the missing numbers.

a) 3 × 2 = 6 30 × 2 = ☐ ☐ × 2 = 600 60 ÷ ☐ = 2

b) 4 × 7 = 28 4 × ☐ = 280 400 × 7 = ☐

5 marks

PS 2. Maya says, '30 has only two factor pairs, 30 × 1 and 15 × 2'.
Do you agree? Explain your answer.

____

____

1 mark

Total: ☐ /37 marks

Had a go ☐ **Getting there** ☐ **Got it!** ☐

Written methods for multiplication and division

- Multiply 2-digit and 3-digit numbers by a 1-digit number using short multiplication
- Divide 2-digit and 3-digit numbers by a 1-digit number using short division

Short multiplication

Examples

Calculate 53 × 6

		5	3
×			6
	3	1	8
		1	

Step 1: Write the **multiplication** out in columns with the 1-digit put under the ones column
Step 2: Multiply the ones by the 1-digit number and carry the tens over to the tens column
Step 3: Multiply the tens by the 1-digit number and add any carried tens

So, 53 × 6 = 318

Calculate 784 × 3

	7	8	4
×			3
2	3	5	2
	2	1	

Step 1: Write the multiplication out in columns with the 1-digit put under the ones column
Step 2: Multiply the ones by the 1-digit number and carry the tens over to the tens column
Step 3: Multiply the tens by the 1-digit number and add any carried tens
Step 4: Multiply the hundreds by the 1-digit number and add any carried hundreds

So, 784 × 3 = 2,352

Short division

Example

Calculate 456 ÷ 3

	1	5	2
3	4	[1]5	6

Step 1: Write the **division** as a 'bus stop'. Look at the first number, 4: 4 ÷ 3 = 1 remainder 1. Write 1 above the line (in the hundreds column, which represents 100) and write 1, (which represents 10) next to the second number, 5
Step 2: Now look at the 5 and the carried figure, which together gives 15: 15 ÷ 3 = 5. Write 5 above the line in the tens column (which represents 50)
Step 3: Now look at 6: 6 ÷ 3 = 2. Write 2 above the line (in the ones column)

So, 456 ÷ 3 = 152

Remember

The dividend (number to be divided) is placed under the 'bus stop'. The divisor (number it is to be divided by) is put on the left-hand side of the 'bus stop'.
This method is also known as short division.

Key words

- multiplication
- division

Challenge 1

1. Complete the calculations using short multiplication.

a) 68×3 = ______

b) 74×4 = ______

c) 58×6 = ______

d) 324×7 = ______

e) 108×4 = ______

f) 467×4 = ______

6 marks

2. Complete the calculations using short division.

a) $5 \overline{)65}$

b) $4 \overline{)68}$

c) $7 \overline{)91}$

d) $3 \overline{)861}$

e) $4 \overline{)792}$

f) $8 \overline{)912}$

6 marks

Challenge 2

PS 1. Fill in the missing numbers.

a) 2 ☐ 3 × 5 = 1215

b) ☐ 3 ☐ × 7 = 3031

3 marks

Challenge 3

PS 1. Write **true** or **false** for each statement.

a) 156 × 7 is less than 204 × 3 ______

b) 496 ÷ 4 is more than 98 × 3 ______

2 marks

PS 2. Arun says 321 ÷ 3 is the same as 152 × 3. Do you agree? Explain your answer.

______

______

1 mark

Total: ☐ / 18 marks

Had a go ☐ Getting there ☐ Got it! ☐

Multiplication and division word problems

- Solve one-step and two-step multiplication and division word problems
- Solve correspondence problems

Word problem

Example

The jug holds 750 millilitres of orange juice. How much juice can be poured **equally** into each glass?

$$5\,\overline{)\,7\;{}^{2}5\;0\,}\quad\text{answer: } 1\;5\;0$$

So, there are 150 millilitres for each glass.

To solve this problem, you first should decide if you need to multiply or divide. When you read the problem, you can interpret that you need to pour the total amount of juice equally into 5 glasses, so this means we need to divide 750 by 5.

Scaling problem

Example

These are the ingredients needed to make one smoothie:

- 1 ripe banana • 145 g mixed berries • 3 spoons of yoghurt

Toby wants to make four smoothies. How many grams of mixed berries will he need?

$$\begin{array}{r} 1\;4\;5 \\ \times \quad\;\; 4 \\ \hline 5\;8\;0 \\ \hline {\scriptstyle 1\;\;2\;\;} \end{array}$$

So, Toby needs 580 g of berries to make four smoothies.

To solve this problem, first you need to decide if you need to multiply or divide. You need to find how many grams of berries are needed for four smoothies, so this means we need to multiply the amount of berries (145 g) by 4.

Correspondence problem

Example

Shivi is making a pizza. He can choose two toppings from the selection to put on his tomato base.
Selection of toppings: mushrooms, peppers, olives, ham.
List all the different pizzas Shivi could make.

Pizza 1	mushrooms	peppers
Pizza 2	mushrooms	olives
Pizza 3	mushrooms	ham
Pizza 4	peppers	olives
Pizza 5	peppers	ham
Pizza 6	olives	ham

To solve this problem, it is best to draw a table. First, choose one topping from the list (e.g. mushrooms) and then match it with each of the other three different toppings (e.g. peppers, olives and ham). Then choose the next topping and match it to the other toppings on the **list**. And so on. Make sure you are **systematic** and remember to delete any repeated combinations. For example, mushrooms and peppers is the same as peppers and mushrooms.

Key words

- equal
- systematic

Challenge 1

1. The length of a table is 345 cm. The length of the room is 4 times longer than the table. What is the length of the room? [ ] cm

1 mark

2. 252 players are at a netball tournament. There are 9 players in each netball team. How many teams are at the tournament? [ ]

1 mark

3. An elephant eats 205 kg of vegetation in one day. How much vegetation would you expect the elephant to eat in seven days? [ ] kg

1 mark

Challenge 2

PS 1. Ted has four pairs of socks: 1 red pair, 1 blue pair, 1 black pair and 1 green pair.

Ted has two pairs of trainers: 1 grey pair and 1 white pair.

Complete the table to show all possible combinations of socks and trainers.

Trainers	Socks

8 marks

Challenge 3

PS 1. There are 9 classrooms in a school. In each classroom, there are 8 table pots with 36 colouring pencils in each pot. How many colouring pencils are there in total in all the classrooms? Show your working.

2 marks

PS 2. A café ordered 6 boxes of strawberry yoghurt with 64 yoghurt pots in each box, and 4 boxes of cherry yoghurt with 78 yoghurt pots in each box. How many yoghurt pots did the café order in total? Show your working.

2 marks

Total: [ ] / 15 marks

Had a go [ ] **Getting there** [ ] **Got it!** [ ]

Progress test 2

1. **Use the number cards to make this number sentence correct.**

204 1,412

________ > 290 > 250 > ________

2 marks

PS 2. **Marco and Sarah are playing a computer game.**

Marco scores 1,545 points on the game.

Sarah scores 472 points on the game.

How many points do they score in total? ☐

1 mark

3. **Write the number shown on the place value chart in words.**

Thousands	Hundreds	Tens	Ones
1,000	100	10 10	1 1

____

1 mark

PS 4. Complete the **missing numbers** in this multiplication grid.

×	3	4	5
4	12		20
	18	24	30
8		32	

4 marks

PS 5. **Here is a table showing the temperature in two different cities.**

City	Temperature
London	−2°C
Rome	9°C

a) The temperature in Lisbon is 8°C warmer than in London. What is the temperature in Lisbon? ☐ °C

b) What is the difference between the temperature in London and Rome?

☐ °C

2 marks

PS 6. 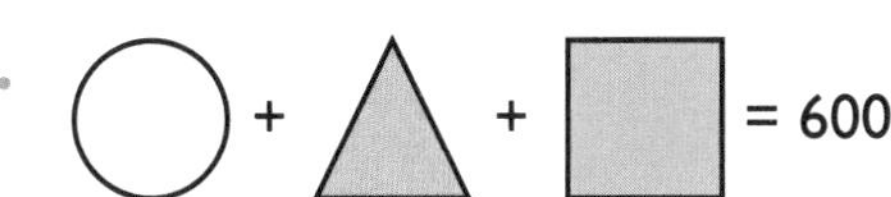 = 600

The value of the square is 375.

The value of the circle is 125.

Write the value of the triangle. ☐

1 mark

PS 7. **Arun has 107 stickers in each of his sticker albums.**

He has 4 albums.

How many stickers does he have altogether? ☐

1 mark

8. **Use <, > or = to complete the statements.**

a) 36 ÷ 6 ☐ 6 × 6

b) 6 ÷ 1 ☐ 6 × 0

c) 60 ÷ 2 ☐ 6 × 20

3 marks

9. **This table shows the lengths of some of the longest rivers in the world.**

Complete the table.

Name of river	Length	Rounded to the nearest 1,000 km
Amazon	6,400 km	a)
Nile	6,695 km	b)
Congo	4,700 km	c)

3 marks

10. Complete the calculations.

a)

	Th	H	T	O
	2	2	2	1
+	3	4	3	9

b)

	Th	H	T	O
	5	8	3	7
−	2	5	7	2

2 marks

PS **11. Use these four digits to write the smallest possible number.**

7 1 1 2 [ ]

1 mark

12. Circle the calculations that give the same answer to 3 × 4 × 5.

4 × 5 × 4 20 × 3 6 × 4 × 2 6 × 12 6 × 10 × 1

2 marks

13. Write the number 50 using Roman numerals.

____

1 mark

PS **14. Apple juice is delivered in boxes of six bottles. The local café orders 84 bottles.**

How many boxes will be delivered? [ ]

1 mark

15. Here are six numbers.

6,568 7,981 3,540 1,320 5,567 7,993

Write the numbers in **ascending** order.

____

1 mark

PS **16. List all the factor pairs of 48.**

____

1 mark

PS **17. Katya says, '100 is a multiple of 25, so all multiples of 25 are even numbers'. Do you agree? Explain your answer.**

____

____

1 mark

PS 18. This table shows the height of three different planes in the sky.

Plane	Height in metres
GoJet	6,654
EasyAir	6,540
SkyOrange	6,855

How much lower is SkyOrange than the combined height of the other two planes? Show your working.

2 marks

PS 19. For lunch at school on Monday, there is a choice of chicken or tofu for the main course and a choice of an apple or ice cream for pudding.

Write all the different possible combinations of a main course and pudding.

4 marks

PS 20. Write the missing numbers in this calculation.

	5	7	9	1
	2	4	2	☐
+	3	☐	7	7
1	2	0	8	9

2 marks

Total: ☐ / 36 marks

Handwriting and homophones

- Use diagonal and horizontal strokes needed to join letters
- Spell homophones and near-homophones accurately

Homophones

Homophones are words that sound exactly the same but use different letters. When using homophones it is important to spell the word correctly to avoid confusing the meaning.

Handwriting

As well as joining letters using cursive handwriting, it is also important to make sure letters have consistent size and orientation. This is especially important with letters with **ascenders** (parts that rise above the main part of the letter) and **descenders** (parts that extend below the main part of the letter).

Practising the formation of the individual letters should then be followed by joining the letters together.

Remember

When practising handwriting, make sure that you are sitting comfortably at a table and holding your pen or pencil correctly.

Example

Look at how the size of the letters is consistent in each pair of homophones below. Notice how the ascenders and descenders have the same direction and length.

Practise copying these words using cursive writing. Use a dictionary if you are unsure of any of the word meanings.

heal	heel	meat	meet
meddle	medal	grate	great
weather	whether	piece	peace
whose	who's	accept	except
mail	male	fair	fare

Key words

- homophones
- ascender
- descender

Challenge 1

1. Using joined handwriting, write each word several times to practise keeping ascenders and descenders consistent.

happy ______________________________

school ______________________________

heard ______________________________

believe ______________________________

probably ______________________________

naughty ______________________________

6 marks

Challenge 2

1. Write a definition of each word using joined handwriting.

scene ______________________________

____

seen ______________________________

____

meat ______________________________

____

meet ______________________________

____

rein ______________________________

____

rain ______________________________

____

6 marks

Challenge 3

1. Write two sentences that show the difference between the words **missed** and **mist**, using joined handwriting.

____

____

____

2 marks

Total: / 14 marks

Had a go ☐ **Getting there** ☐ **Got it!** ☐

Prefixes

- Accurately use the prefixes **in-**, **il-**, **im-** and **ir-**

in- meaning not

The **prefix in-** normally means 'not' although it can occasionally mean 'in' or 'into'.

Example

inactive means not active

They were inactive because they were sitting watching TV.

independent means not dependent

I did the independent work. I was not dependent on my teacher for help with it.

Sometimes the **in-** needs to be changed depending on the letters that follow it.

Example

- If the **root word** starts with **r** then **in** is changed to **ir**
  - regular becomes **ir**regular (not inregular)
  - relevant becomes **ir**relevant

  The shape was an irregular pentagon.

  The weather was irrelevant as they would run anyway.

- If the root word starts with **l** then **in** becomes **il**
  - legal becomes **il**legal (not inlegal)
  - legible becomes **il**legible

  It was illegal to drive on the right-hand side of the road.

  His handwriting was illegible.

- If the root word starts with **p** or **m** then **in** becomes **im**
  - possible becomes **im**possible (not inpossible)
  - mature becomes **im**mature

  The boy found it impossible to climb over the wall.

  *Throwing the toy was **im**mature.*

Key words

- prefix
- root word

Challenge 1

1. Draw a line from each prefix to the correct root word.

im- **il-** **in-** **inter-** **ir-**

national regular mortal legal correct

5 marks

Challenge 2

1. Choose the correct word to complete each sentence.

irresponsible **imperfect** **impatient** **inactive** **illegal**

a) It is very ________________ to play in the road.

b) Conor was waiting for his mum and he was very ________________.

c) Gran gets a stiff back if she is ________________ for too long.

d) It is ________________ to steal things.

e) The cake was tasty even though it was ________________.

5 marks

Challenge 3

1. Circle the incorrectly spelled words and then explain what is wrong with their spelling.

inregular **immortal** **ilpossible** **imcorrect** **irrelevant**

____

____

____

3 marks

2. Complete each sentence with the correct prefix added to the underlined word to give the opposite meaning.

a) Their argument was ______logical.

b) The measurements were very ______accurate.

2 marks

Total: / 15 marks

Had a go **Getting there** **Got it!**

Word endings -sure and -ture

- Correctly spell words with -sure and -ture endings

-sure endings

Care is needed with the spelling of **word endings**.

Words that have the same sound at the end, such as the word **treasure**, often have the **sure** spelling.

Example

mea**sure**	*Measure the ingredients carefully.*
lei**sure**	*Walking is my main leisure activity.*
plea**sure**	*It was a great pleasure to see so many friends.*
enclo**sure**	*The animals were kept in a large enclosure.*

-ture endings

Words that have the same sound at the end of them as in the word **picture** often have the **ture** spelling.

Example

crea**ture**	*My favourite creature is the octopus.*
fea**ture**	*His poem will feature in the school magazine.*
furni**ture**	*Sophie had new bedroom furniture.*
struc**ture**	*The bridge is a magnificent structure.*

Tip

Think whether there is a root word that may influence the ending you place on a word.

Exceptions

There are exceptions so care is needed with word endings. Some words that rhyme with **picture** and **creature** do not have the **ture** ending. If the root word ends in **ch** or **tch** then the ending will be **-er**.

Example

tea**ch** → teach**er**
stre**tch** → stretch**er**
ri**ch** → rich**er**

Key word

- word ending

Challenge 1

1. Complete each word using the correct ending.

a) mea______________

b) struc______________

c) depar______________

d) lei______________

4 marks

Challenge 2

1. Choose the correct word to add into each sentence.

mixture **creature** **adventure** **pleasure**

a) They packed their backpacks and set off on an ______________.

b) Nobody knew what the strange, furry ______________ was.

c) She got ______________ from giving presents.

d) All the ingredients stirred together made the cake ______________.

4 marks

Challenge 3

1. Write a sentence using each word.

a) structure ____________________________

____

b) feature ____________________________

____

c) measure ____________________________

____

d) departure ____________________________

____

e) fixture ____________________________

____

5 marks

Total: ☐ / 13 marks

Had a go ☐ **Getting there** ☐ **Got it!** ☐

Word endings sounding like zhun

- Correctly spell words with endings sounding like zhun

zhun sound endings

For many verbs ending in **se** or **de**, changing the spelling of the **word ending** to **-sion** results in a **zhun** sound.

Example

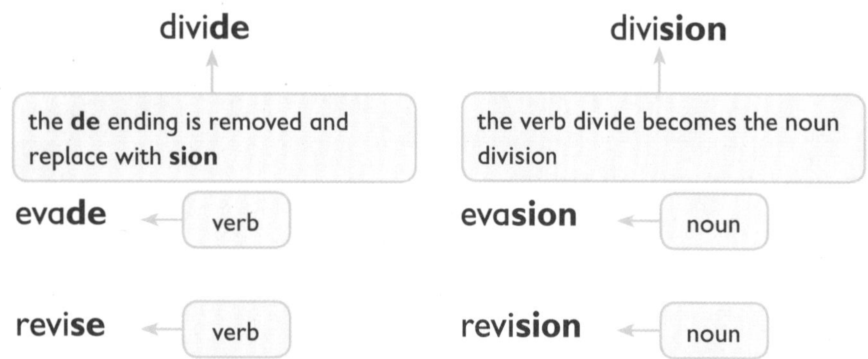

Care must be taken though as there are exceptions.

Example

- **tense** ends in **se** and ten**sion** is spelled with **sion**, but the word makes a shun sound rather than zhun.

The shun sound has a different spelling and some of the spellings must be avoided when spelling zhun sounding words.

Example

admi**ssion** ⟶ the **ssion** makes a shun sound
musi**cian** ⟶ the **cian** makes a shun sound
ac**tion** ⟶ the **tion** makes a shun sound

Remember

Word endings often depend on the spelling of the root word.

Key word

- word ending

Challenge 1

1. Read each word below and write it in the correct place in the table depending on the sound it has at the end.

erosion **admission** **evasion** **tension** **mansion**
vision **musician** **illusion**

zhun ending (as in division)	**shun** ending (as in action)

8 marks

Challenge 2

1. Change the following verbs to nouns with **-sion** endings.

a) invade ______________

b) conclude ______________

c) confuse ______________

d) collide ______________

e) exclude ______________

f) delude ______________

6 marks

Challenge 3

1. Write a sentence for each word.

a) erosion ______________________________

____

b) decision ______________________________

____

c) collision ______________________________

____

d) confusion ______________________________

____

4 marks

Total: ☐ / 18 marks

Had a go ☐ Getting there ☐ Got it! ☐

Settings, characters and plot

- Create settings, characters and plot

Building a story

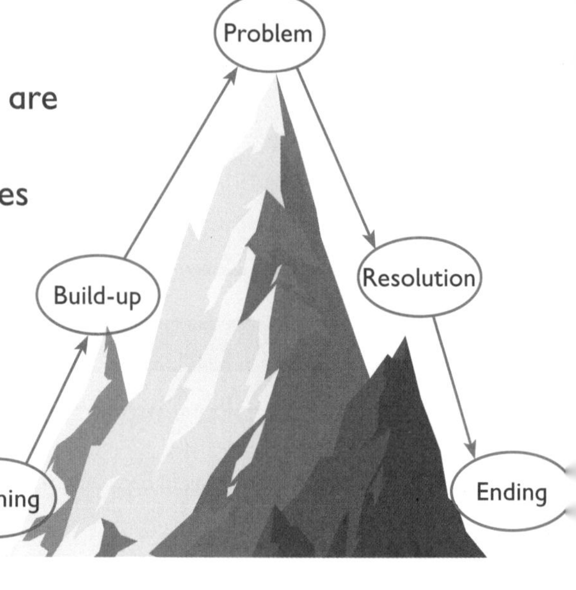

Composition is all about putting a text together. There are many parts that make texts successful.

- The **opening** often describes the setting and introduces characters.
- The **build-up** will usually have some action – what characters are doing and feeling as a **plot** develops – and can introduce the problem.
- The **problem** is an issue the character(s) need to overcome.
- The **resolution** tells the reader what the character(s) do in overcoming the problem. It might reveal why the problem occurred in the first place.
- The **ending** will usually have a good or bad outcome, finishing the story in a neat and tidy way.

Composing a story

Each section of the story contains sentences that describe **characters** and **setting**, and tell the reader what happens.

Example

Opening
It was a cold, dull morning. The small bedroom was freezing. Denzel slowly got out of bed. He was nine years old and did not like mornings.

Build-up
He was already late and still had to get ready for school. It was nearly time to meet his friends, so he dressed quicker than usual. As always, he looked out of the window to see where they were. Denzel held his breath. There was nothing out there.

Problem
No garden, no car, no road, no houses. Just plain grey emptiness.

Remember

Use of adjectives and adverbs will help characters and settings come alive for the reader.

Tip

Think about stories you have read. How are characters and settings described? How do plots develop?

Key words

- composition
- plot
- character
- setting

Read the story outline again and answer the questions in Challenges 1 to 3.

Opening: It was a cold, dull morning. The small bedroom was freezing. Denzel slowly got out of bed. He was nine years old and did not like mornings.

Build-up: He was already late and still had to get ready for school. It was nearly time to meet his friends, so he dressed quicker than usual. As always, he looked out of the window to see where they were. Denzel held his breath. There was nothing out there.

Problem: No garden, no car, no road, no houses. Just plain grey emptiness.

Challenge 1

1. Read the story **opening**. Write two more sentences describing Denzel.

____

____

____

4 marks

Challenge 2

1. Read the **problem** section of the story. Write two more sentences to further describe what Denzel saw.

____

____

____

4 marks

Challenge 3

1. Think about the story and develop the plot by making notes to plan what might happen in the **resolution** and **ending** sections.

Resolution	Ending

4 marks

Total: ☐ / 12 marks

Had a go ☐ **Getting there** ☐ **Got it!** ☐

Writing – Composition

Organising writing

- Organise writing in paragraphs

Paragraphs

Paragraphs are important organisational features of a text. If sentences are written without paragraphs, a text can be more difficult to read.

Example

They had enjoyed the hockey match. The children played well and deserved their medal. The disco was great fun. Dan won the dancing competition. Kelly helped sell drinks and snacks. Soft bedsheets were very welcome that night. It had been a busy, tiring day and they would sleep well.

The sentences above are all about two children, Dan and Kelly, and they make sense. However, the sentences are about three different parts of the children's day, so they would be better split into paragraphs:

- **Paragraph 1** about the hockey match – 'They had enjoyed …'
- **Paragraph 2** about the disco – 'The disco was great fun …'
- **Paragraph 3** about them being tired – 'Soft bedsheets …'

As more information is added to a text, paragraphs become longer and can also be split into further paragraphs.

Example

The disco was great fun. The music was loud and Dan got his chance to show off some amazing dancing moves. At the end of the evening he was awarded the prize for best dancer.

Kelly did not feel like dancing. She helped Miss Green to sell refreshments. They managed to sell all the crisps and sweets and most of the drinks, raising over £200 for charity.

The paragraph about the disco has been split into two paragraphs, one giving detail about Dan and his dancing, and the other about Kelly selling refreshments.

Remember

When planning writing, it is useful to think about what information each paragraph will contain.

Tip

Make a list of some of the ideas you want to include in each paragraph before you start writing.

Key word

- paragraph

Challenge 1

1. Read the text below. It could be split into three paragraphs. Write the first three words of the sentence that starts each paragraph.

> The puppy was only 12 weeks old. It had soft fur and wore a red collar. Lois had wanted a pet for a long time. She had asked for a goldfish, a hamster, a rat and a kitten. Anything would do, she thought. She hadn't even got round to asking for a puppy. Mum had made a special den under the stairs. Lois had not realised what she was doing. This is where the puppy would sleep.

Paragraph 1: ______ ______ ______

Paragraph 2: ______ ______ ______

Paragraph 3: ______ ______ ______

3 marks

Read the text below that has one paragraph and answer the questions in challenges 2 and 3.

> Eva enjoyed school. She enjoyed most lessons. Music and PE were her favourites. She did not like Art. She had lots of friends and always sat with them for lunch.

Challenge 2

1. Rewrite the text. Split the text into two paragraphs and add at least one more sentence to each paragraph.

______

______

______

______

4 marks

Challenge 3

1. Explain why you have chosen to split the text above in the way you have.

______

______

______

2 marks

Total: ☐ /9 marks

Had a go ☐ **Getting there** ☐ **Got it!** ☐

Writing – Composition

Organising non-fiction writing

- Using paragraphs in non-fiction writing

Non-fiction texts

Non-fiction texts often use subheadings to organise information. There will then be at least one **paragraph** related to that information.

Example

Subheading – what this section of text is about

Heading – what the text is about

The R101

Enormous luxury

The R101 was a fine machine. It was designed to carry passengers across oceans in posh cabins and serve them fine food as it cruised serenely through the air.

A paragraph about luxury

At over 220 m long, it was the largest airship built at the time. It was so big that the Titanic would have fitted inside it.

The R101 needed to be big. Inside its vast shell were 15 huge bags of hydrogen gas used to lift it into the air.

Two paragraphs about the airship's size

The huge British airship the R101, crashed on its maiden voyage in 1930, claiming the lives of 48 people.

Planning

It is important to **plan** non-fiction texts carefully.

Example

Subheading – **Enormous luxury**	Paragraph 1 – about luxury Paragraph 2 – size of the airship Paragraph 3 – why it was so big
Subheading – **First voyage**	Paragraph 1 – when it happened Paragraph 2 – where it was going
Subheading – **Disaster**	Paragraph 1 – what happened to the R101 Paragraph 2 – the reason it crashed

Tip

Thinking about each subheading can help with thinking about what information is needed in each paragraph.

Key words

- paragraph
- plan

Challenge 1

1. Match each piece of information to the paragraph in which it would be written.

Paragraph 1 – about choosing tropical fish	Paragraph 2 – about where to keep tropical fish	Paragraph 3 – about caring for the fish
water temperature	different types of tropical fish	choosing a fish tank

3 marks

Challenge 2

1. Here is a plan for a piece of writing about school. Think of a suitable name for each subheading.

Subheading	Paragraph
a) ______	Paragraph 1 – who my teacher is Paragraph 2 – who I sit with Paragraph 3 – our classroom
b) ______	Paragraph 1 – subjects in the morning Paragraph 2 – subjects in the afternoon

2 marks

Challenge 3

1. For each subheading in a piece of writing about yourself, write a brief description of the information you might include in each paragraph.

Subheading	Paragraph
a) Family	1 ______ 2 ______
b) Hobbies	1 ______ 2 ______
c) When I grow up	1 ______ 2 ______

6 marks

Total: / 11 marks

Had a go **Getting there** **Got it!**

Checking and developing writing

- Proofread writing for spelling and punctuation errors
- Suggest improvements to the effectiveness of writing during editing

Improving writing

When writing, it is important to check or **proofread** what you have written to make sure there are no spelling mistakes and that no punctuation is missing.

It is also important to **edit** writing, making changes if it can be improved.

Ask:

- Does it make sense?
- Could more effective words be used?
- Could sentences sound better?

Remember

Interesting words and sentences grab the reader's attention.

Example

A fronted adverbial may sound better here, e.g. After school, we went to the café.

Capital letter for name – Jess

This sentence doesn't sound right. Try: As we chatted we overheard a man at the next table. He was wearing sunglasses and had a mean grin.

This is a response to a question so use 'replied' instead of 'said'.

We went to the café after school. I got a big milkshake for my friend jess. We were chatting away when we overheard a man at the next table with sunglasses and mean grin.

You wait in the car and I will go in to get the money, he said.

The person he was sitting with said, yes that sounds like a good plan.

When they stood up to leave, we followed them Jess took a photo of their car and I called the police.

Use 'bought' instead of 'got', and 'large' instead of 'big'.

Inverted commas are missing from both spoken parts.

Be more specific – Man? Woman?

Missing full stop

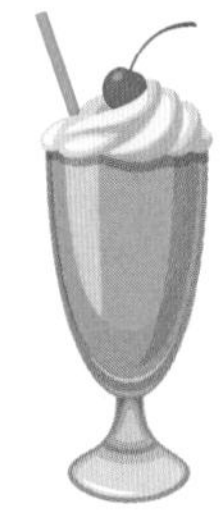

Key words

- proofreading
- editing

When proofreading, it is often a good idea to read aloud to hear how each sentence sounds.

Challenge 1

1. Choose a more effective word for each of the adverbs and adjectives underlined in the text below.

The <u>nice</u> horse galloped <u>well</u> along the road. As the <u>bright</u> sun beat down, the children held on <u>carefully</u>. The <u>big</u> desert lay before them.

5 marks

Read the passage below and answer the questions in Challenges 2 and 3:

The horse did not slow as the sun moved closer to the horizon Shadows grew longer and dusk became knight. Onwards they sped, towards the dark shape of mountins in the distance. There amazing beast kept going although it was getting tired. each child starred at the stars. They saw familiar shapes in the heavens and knew they were nearly their.

Challenge 2

1. Circle each of the spelling and punctuation errors in the text.

7 marks

Challenge 3

1. Rewrite the first and fourth sentences, starting them with the given words.

First sentence: As...

____

____

Fourth sentence: Although...

____

____

2 marks

Total: ☐ / 14 marks

Had a go ☐ **Getting there** ☐ **Got it!** ☐

Progress test 3

1. **Read the poem and then answer the questions.**

Patience

Waiting,
Still and silent.
Staring at the soft, white,
Squeezing from the machine.
Those few seconds,
Seem like a lifetime.
When you really want,
To eat ice-cream.

a) Why is this poem called *Patience*? ____________________

b) *'Those few seconds, Seem like a lifetime.'* What do these words mean?

____

c) Why do you think the poet leaves it to the end of the poem to mention ice-cream?

____

3 marks

2. **Match each word to its meaning.**

a) descend	to go up
b) fascinating	a view or place
c) scene	to go down
d) ascend	very interesting

4 marks

3. **Copy each word three times using joined handwriting to practise keeping ascenders and descenders consistent.**

disobey ______ ______ ______

simply ______ ______ ______

league ______ ______ ______

tongue __________ __________ __________

weigh __________ __________ __________

pleasure __________ __________ __________

6 marks

4. Choose the correct word to complete each sentence.

immature impossible illegible irregular irrelevant

a) His handwriting was __________.

b) The maths homework seemed __________ at first.

c) Gran said Grandad was __________ because he was playing with some children's toys.

d) I love cheese so the type is __________.

e) The shop opening times are __________ as they change all the time.

5 marks

5. Write a sentence using each word correctly.

a) invasion __________

b) decision __________

c) confusion __________

d) explosion __________

e) collision __________

5 marks

6. **Add the correct -sure or -ture ending to each word.**

a) trea________________

b) depar________________

c) na________________

d) enclo________________

e) mea________________

f) pic________________

6 marks

7. **Think about the story of Cinderella. She lost her slipper at the ball and the Prince did not know who she was or where she lived to be able to return it and see her again.**

a) Make notes to show how this problem is resolved and what happens at the end of the story.

Resolution	Ending

2 marks

b) Write a description of the glass slipper. Think about what it looked like and how it felt in the Prince's hands.

____

____

____

____

2 marks

8. Read the text below that has only one paragraph.

They have been flying kites for three years. Lucy and her dad had already made a small kite together and they decided to make an even better one. Every week they go to Kite Club where they fly kites with other people and put on displays. Even if there is not enough wind to fly, they still go and make new kites.

Rewrite the text, splitting it into two paragraphs and add at least one more sentence to each paragraph.

____

____

____

____

____

____

____

4 marks

9. Choose a more effective word for each of the adverbs and adjectives underlined in the text below.

The car was <u>shiny</u> and it made a <u>big</u> roar when they started the engine.

It looked <u>fast</u> but when it raced it was very slow. Tilly thought there was

something wrong with the engine. Mum had a <u>lovely</u> tool kit. She was a <u>good</u>

mechanic and soon had the engine apart. Tilly <u>looked</u> in amazement.

6 marks

Total: ☐ /43 marks

Recognising fractions and equivalent fractions

- Recognise and show equivalent fractions
- Find fractions of amounts

Equivalent fractions

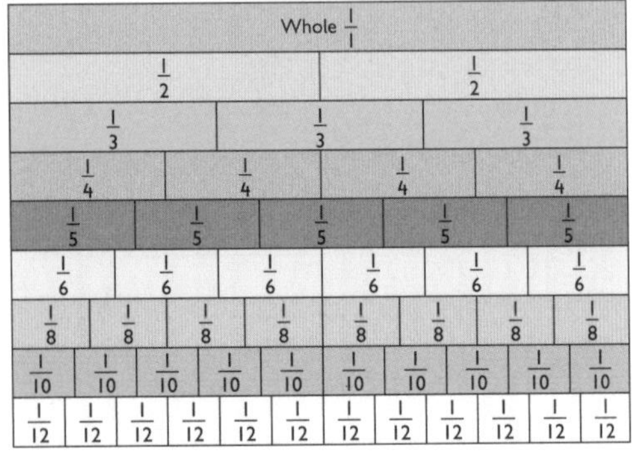

You can use the **fraction wall** to find **equivalent** fractions.

$\frac{1}{2} = \frac{2}{4}$ $\quad$ $\frac{3}{6} = \frac{6}{12}$

$\frac{2}{4} = \frac{4}{8}$ $\quad$ $\frac{2}{5} = \frac{4}{10}$

$\frac{1}{2} = \frac{3}{6}$ $\quad$ $\frac{2}{4} = \frac{5}{10}$

Tip

Notice that when we are adding or subtracting fractions, the **numerator** changes but the **denominator** always stays the same.

Adding and subtracting fractions

Example

Calculate $\frac{8}{12} + \frac{6}{12}$

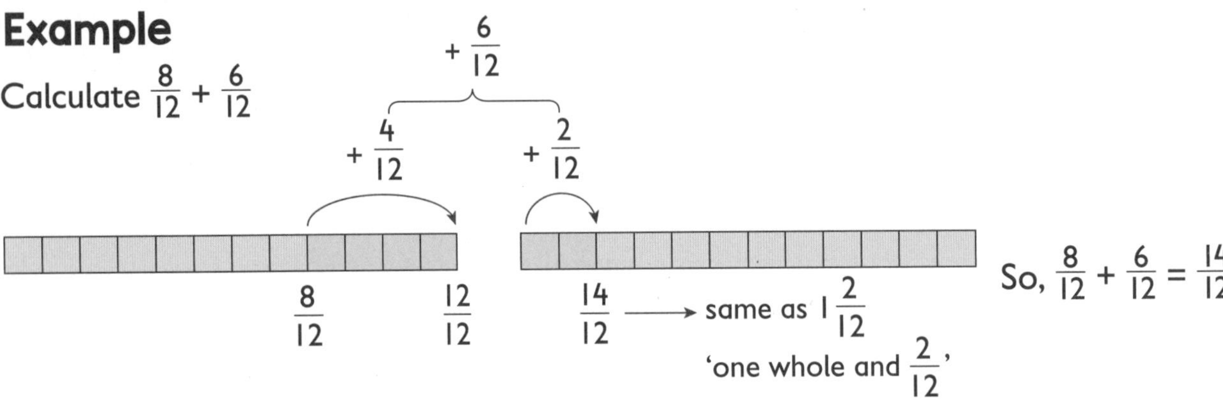

So, $\frac{8}{12} + \frac{6}{12} = \frac{14}{12}$

Subtract $\frac{7}{10} - \frac{4}{10}$

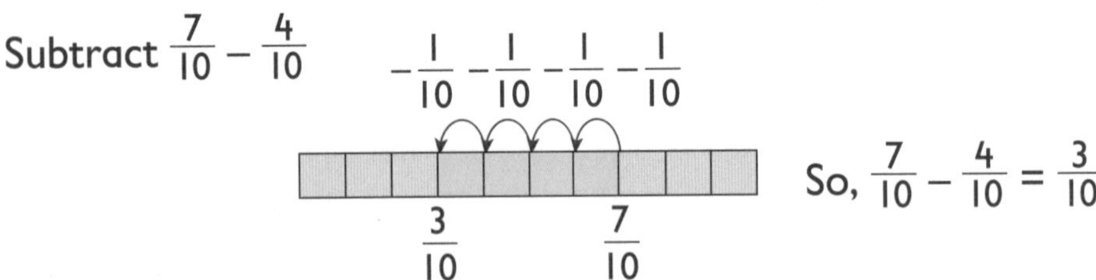

So, $\frac{7}{10} - \frac{4}{10} = \frac{3}{10}$

Fractions of amounts

A fifth ($\frac{1}{5}$) means dividing something into 5 **equal parts**.

Example

Calculate $\frac{4}{5}$ of 60.

You can use a bar model:

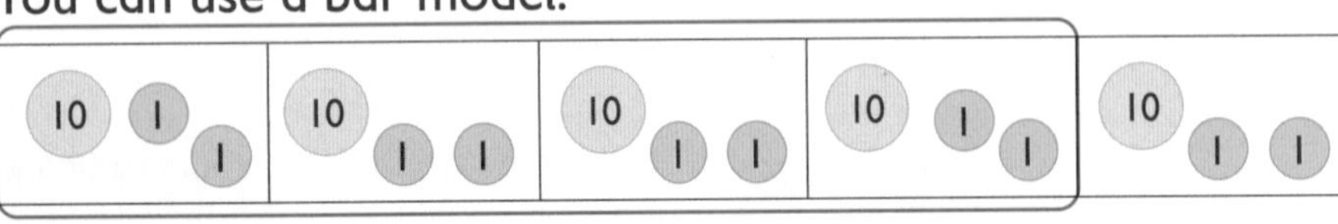

$\frac{4}{5}$ of 60 = 48

Key words

- fraction
- equivalent
- numerator
- denominator
- equal
- part

Challenge 1

1. Complete the fraction sentences.

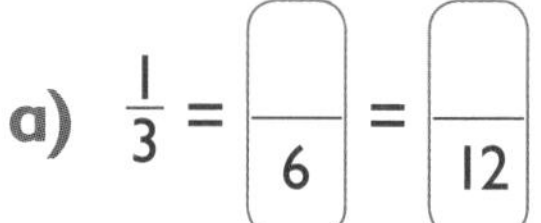

a) $\frac{1}{3} = \frac{\square}{6} = \frac{\square}{12}$ b) $\frac{\square}{2} = \frac{2}{4} = \frac{\square}{8}$ c) $\frac{3}{\square} = \frac{\square}{10}$ d) $\frac{\square}{12} = \frac{3}{4} = \frac{\square}{8}$

8 marks

2. Complete the fraction calculations.

a) $\frac{3}{10} + \frac{2}{10} = \frac{\square}{\square}$ b) $\frac{5}{6} + \frac{4}{6} = \frac{\square}{\square}$ c) $\frac{8}{12} - \frac{2}{12} = \frac{\square}{\square}$

d) $\frac{4}{8} + \frac{\square}{\square} = 1\frac{3}{8}$ e) $\frac{4}{5} + \frac{2}{5} + \frac{3}{5} = \frac{\square}{\square}$ f) $1 - \frac{4}{7} = \frac{\square}{\square}$

6 marks

Challenge 2

1. Use this bar model to answer these calculations.

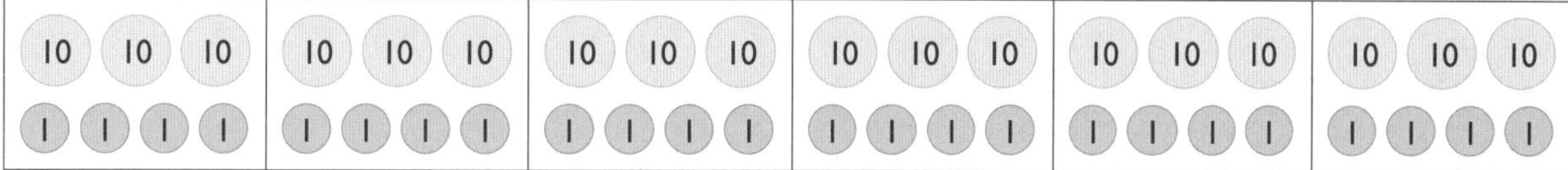

10 10 10 1 1 1 1	10 10 10 1 1 1 1	10 10 10 1 1 1 1	10 10 10 1 1 1 1	10 10 10 1 1 1 1	10 10 10 1 1 1 1

a) $\frac{2}{6}$ of 204 = ☐ b) $\frac{4}{6}$ of 204 = ☐ c) $\frac{5}{6}$ of 204 = ☐

3 marks

PS 2. Jen has £750 in her bank account. She uses $\frac{1}{10}$ of the £750 to buy some new trainers, and $\frac{2}{5}$ of the £750 to buy a new phone. How much money does she have left in her account? ☐

1 mark

PS 3. Jai, Evie and Jo have been cycling round a cycling track. Jai cycled $\frac{6}{9}$, Evie cycled $\frac{8}{9}$ and Jo cycled $\frac{5}{9}$ of the track.

a) How much more did Evie cycle than Jai? $\frac{\square}{\square}$

b) How much less did Jo cycle than Evie? $\frac{\square}{\square}$

c) What is the total amount they all cycled together? $\frac{\square}{\square}$

3 marks

Challenge 3

PS 1. Complete the missing numbers.

a) $\frac{1}{2}$ of ☐ = 75 b) $\frac{3}{4}$ of ☐ = 48 c) $\frac{4}{10}$ of ☐ = 160

3 marks

PS 2. Catalina has taken some money for her trip to the zoo. She spent $\frac{3}{4}$ of her money and has £1.25 left. How much money did she take to the zoo? ☐

1 mark

Total: ☐ **/25 marks**

Had a go ☐ **Getting there** ☐ **Got it!** ☐

Hundredths and dividing by 10 and 100

- Count up and down in hundredths
- Recognise that hundredths arise when dividing an object by one hundred and dividing tenths by ten
- Divide 1-digit or 2-digit numbers by 10 or 100

Recognising hundredths

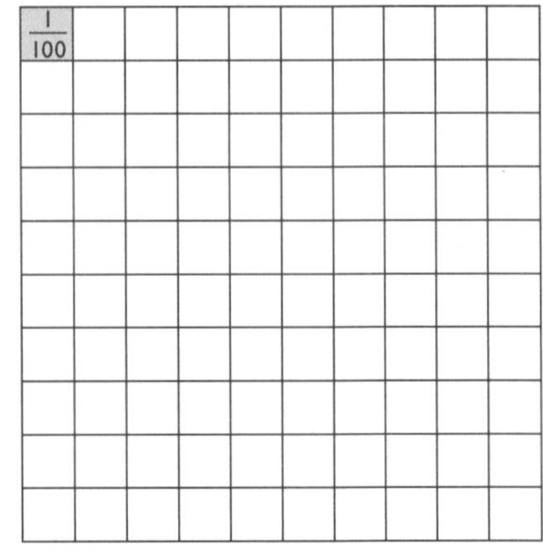

This bar has been divided into ten equal pieces. Each piece is a **tenth**. We write a tenth as $\frac{1}{10}$.

$\frac{1}{10}$									

If we split each tenth into ten equal pieces, then the whole bar is now divided into one hundred equal pieces, so each piece is a **hundredth**. We write a hundredth as $\frac{1}{100}$.

A 1p coin  is a hundredth of £1 . 100 × 1p coins = £1

1 cm is a hundredth of a metre. 100 × 1 cm = 100 cm (1 metre)

Tenths in decimals

When we divide a 1-digit whole number by 10, each digit must move one place to the right. A **decimal point** is used.

Example

4 ÷ 10 = 0.4

	Ones	Decimal point	Tenths
	4	•	0
÷ 10	0	•	4

42 ÷ 10 = 4.2

	Tens	Ones	Decimal point	Tenths
	4	2	•	0
÷ 10		4	•	2

When we divide a 1-digit whole number by 100, each digit must move **two** places to the right.

Example

4 ÷ 100 = 0.04

	Ones	Decimal point	Tenths	Hundredths
	4	•	0	
÷ 100	0	•	0	4

42 ÷ 100 = 0.42

	Tens	Ones	Decimal point	Tenths	Hundredths
	4	2	•	0	
÷ 100		0	•	4	2

Tip

One hundred hundredths make one whole.

Key words

- tenth
- hundredth
- decimal point

Challenge 1

1. Write the missing fractions in the boxes.

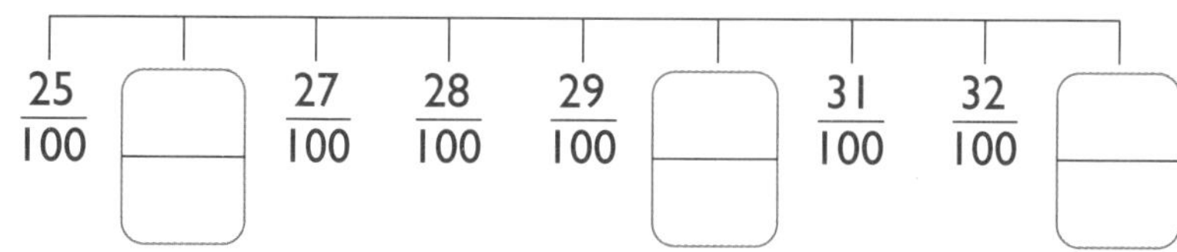

$\frac{25}{100}$ [ ] $\frac{27}{100}$ $\frac{28}{100}$ $\frac{29}{100}$ [ ] $\frac{31}{100}$ $\frac{32}{100}$ [ ]

3 marks

2. Complete the calculations. Use the place value grids to help you.

a) 6 ÷ 10 = [ ]

	Ones	Decimal point	Tenths
	6	•	0
÷ 10		•	

b) 9 ÷ 100 = [ ]

	Ones	Decimal point	Tenths	Hundredths
	9	•	0	
÷ 100		•		

c) 64 ÷ 10 = [ ]

	Tens	Ones	Decimal point	Tenths
	6	4	•	0
÷ 10			•	

d) 78 ÷ 100 = [ ]

	Tens	Ones	Decimal point	Tenths	Hundredths
	7	8	•	0	
÷ 100			•		

4 marks

Challenge 2

1. Circle the calculations that have $\frac{3}{100}$ as the answer.

3 ÷ 10 **30 ÷ 100** **3 ÷ 100** **30 ÷ 10** **0.3 ÷ 10**

1 mark

PS 2. Complete the missing numbers.

a) 6 ÷ [ ] = 0.6 b) 6 ÷ [ ] = 0.06

c) 61 ÷ [ ] = 0.61 d) 11 ÷ [ ] = 1.1

4 marks

Challenge 3

PS 1. A plank of wood measures 75 cm. Joe cuts one hundredth off the plank of wood.

a) How much wood has been cut off? ____________ cm

b) How much wood is left on the plank? ____________ cm

2 marks

Total: [ ] **/ 14 marks**

Had a go [ ] **Getting there** [ ] **Got it!** [ ]

Decimals

- Recognise and write decimal equivalents for fractions
- Round decimals with one decimal place to the nearest whole number
- Compare decimals with the same number of decimal places up to two places

Fraction and decimal equivalents

A fraction is less than one whole. One tenth can be written as a **proper fraction**, $\frac{1}{10}$, or as a decimal fraction (which are just called decimals).

Decimal numbers can be written using a decimal point.

Examples

$\frac{1}{10}$ can be shown as:

Tens	Ones	Decimal point	Tenths	Hundredths
	0	•	1	

$\frac{1}{100}$ can be shown as:

Tens	Ones	Decimal point	Tenths	Hundredths
	0	•	0	1

$\frac{1}{4}$ is the same as $\frac{25}{100}$ so can be shown as:

Tens	Ones	Decimal point	Tenths	Hundredths
	0	•	2	5

Comparing decimals

Decimal numbers can be compared by looking carefully at the place value of each digit.

Example

Which is larger, 1.7 or 1.2?

If you look at the ones they are both the same, so you need to compare the value of the tenths.

7 tenths is more than 2 tenths, so 1.7 is greater than 1.2

Tip

Use a place value grid to help you compare and **round** decimals.

Rounding decimals

Example

Round 1.3 to the nearest whole number.

The value of the tenths is $\frac{3}{10}$, which is less than $\frac{5}{10}$ so you round down to 1.

1 is a **whole number** with no decimal parts.

Key words

- proper fraction
- decimal number
- whole number
- rounding

Challenge 1

1. Write each fraction as a decimal.

a) $\frac{1}{2}$ = ☐ b) $\frac{1}{10}$ = ☐ c) $\frac{3}{4}$ = ☐

d) $\frac{1}{4}$ = ☐ e) $\frac{1}{100}$ = ☐

5 marks

2. Draw a line to match each decimal number to the nearest whole number on the number line.

6.8 **3.5** **1.5** **1.2** **4.9** **5.7** **3.2**

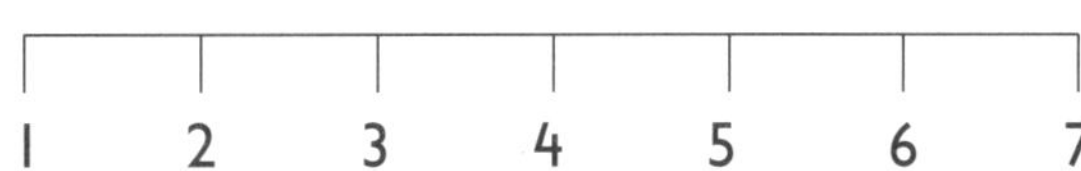

7 marks

Challenge 2

1. Use the symbols < or > between each pair of decimals.

a) 4.9 ☐ 4.2 b) 5.1 ☐ 5.9 c) 7.6 ☐ 8.1

d) 3.5 ☐ 4.6 e) 9 ☐ 8.9 f) 6.8 ☐ 7.5

6 marks

PS 2. Here is a table showing the amount of money raised by three different classes at the school cake sale.

Oak	£43.88
Chestnut	£44.60
Willow	£44.01

Dev says, 'Oak raised the most money and Willow raised the least amount of money'. Do you agree? Explain your answer.

____

____

1 mark

Challenge 3

PS 1. Kaspar jumps 3.7 m in the long jump. How far does he jump to the nearest whole metre? ☐ m

1 mark

PS 2. Jen has these coins in her purse:

Write the amount of money she has in her purse as a decimal amount. £ ☐

1 mark

Total: ☐ /21 marks

Had a go ☐ **Getting there** ☐ **Got it!** ☐

Mixed measures

- Convert between different units of measure
- Estimate, compare and calculate different measures
- Solve simple measure problems involving fractions and decimals to two decimal places

Length

Length is the distance from one end to another end. A ruler or measuring tape is used to measure length. The units for length are **millimetres** (mm), **centimetres** (cm), **metres** (m) and **kilometres** (km).

Remember

It is important to remember key facts:
10 mm = 1 cm
100 cm = 1 m
1,000 m = 1 km

Example

Which length is longest: 1 m, 75 cm or 2.3 m?

1 m = 100 cm; 75 cm = 75 cm; 2.3 m = 2 m and 30 cm = 230 cm

So, the longest length is 2.3 m

To compare each of the three different lengths, you need to **convert** each length into the same unit.

Capacity

Capacity is how much liquid a container can hold. The volume is how much liquid there is in the container. The units for capacity are **litres** (l) and **millilitres** (ml).

Remember

It is important to remember that:
1,000 ml = 1 *l*.

Example

Estimate the capacity of the glass.

You can use your knowledge of other items to help you make a good **estimate**. This glass would hold approximately 200 to 250 ml.

Mass

The **mass** of an object tells us how heavy it is. To measure mass you will need to use a scale. The units for mass are **kilograms** (kg) and **grams** (g).

Remember

It is important to remember that:
1,000 g = 1 kg

Example

One apple weighs 75 g. Ted needs approximately $\frac{1}{2}$ kg of apples to make an apple pie. How many apples does he need?

6 × 75 g = 450 g, 7 × 75 g = 525 g

525 g is closer to approximately $\frac{1}{2}$ kg, which is the same as 500 g, so Ted needs 7 apples.

Key words

- length
- convert
- capacity
- estimate
- mass

Challenge 1

1. Circle the best estimate for each item.

a) A banana weighs: **10 g** **6 kg** **110 g** **275 g**

b) The capacity of a mug: **1 litre** **350 ml** **75 ml** **12.1 ml**

c) The height of a door: **0.5 m** **200 cm** **9 m** **5.2 m**

3 marks

2. Convert each measurement.

a) 4 kg = ☐ g   b) 6.2 *l* = ☐ ml   c) 1.8 km = ☐ m

d) ☐ kg = 500 g   e) ☐ g = 3.7 kg   f) 4.2 m = ☐ cm

6 marks

Challenge 2

1. Write the correct symbol <, > or = between each pair of measurements.

a) 6 kg ☐ 6,000 g   b) 1 km ☐ 100 m   c) $\frac{3}{4}$ m ☐ 750 cm

3 marks

PS 2. Find the difference in kilograms between the sacks of potatoes.

1.2 kg A   750 g B $2\frac{1}{10}$ kg C   1.85 kg D

a) A and C ☐ g   b) B and D ☐ g   c) C and D ☐ g

3 marks

Challenge 3

PS 1. Solve these problems.

a) Mr Chen buys a 500 g tub of butter, a 375 g jar of jam and a 625 g box of cereal. What is the total mass of all three items, in kilograms? ☐ kg

1 mark

b) Dan buys 2 pieces of wood that have a total length of 4.5 m. One length is twice the length of the other. Write the length of each piece of wood.

________ and ________

2 marks

c) A fridge and a freezer are both 520 mm wide. Tim wants to place them side by side in a space that is 1.1 m wide. Beth says it will fit. Do you agree? Explain your answer.

____

____

1 mark

Total: ☐ / 19 marks

Had a go ☐   **Getting there** ☐   **Got it!** ☐

Area and perimeter

- Measure and calculate the perimeter of rectilinear shapes
- Find the area of rectilinear shapes by counting squares
- Solve simple measure problems

Perimeter

Perimeter is the distance or length around a 2-D shape.

Example

Calculate the perimeter of this rectilinear shape.

You need to use a ruler to measure each side of the rectilinear shape and write the measurement next to each side.

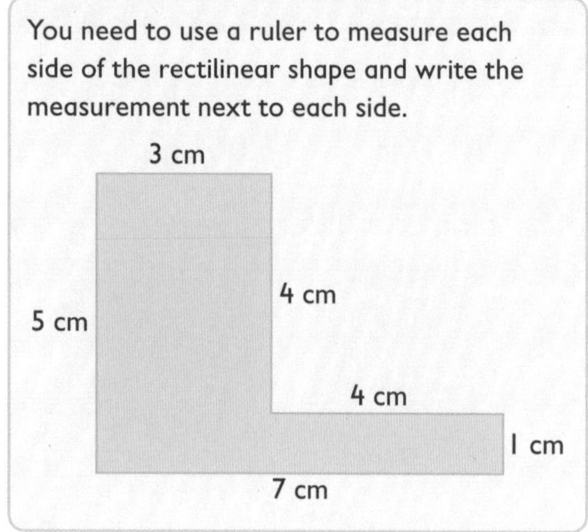

So, to find the perimeter we need to add up the length of each side:
Perimeter = 3 cm + 4 cm + 4 cm + 1 cm + 7 cm + 5 cm = 24 cm

Area

The **area** of a plane shape is the amount of surface it covers. Area is measured in square units.

Example

Calculate the area of this green shape. Each square is 1 cm^2.

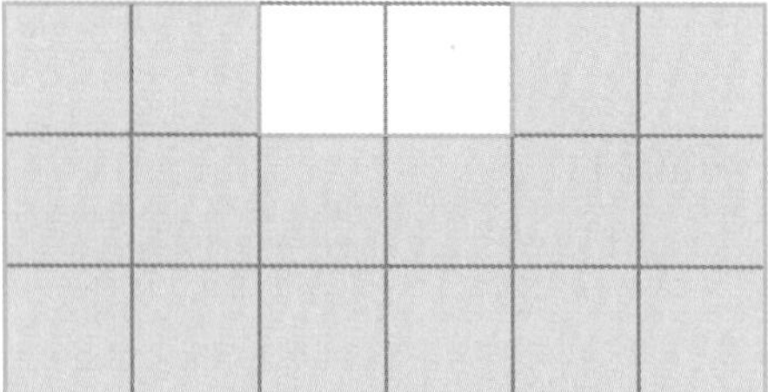

To find the area of the shape, you need to count each square.
The total number of green squares is 16, so the area of the shape is 16 cm^2.

Key words

- perimeter
- area

Challenge 1

1. Use a ruler to find the **perimeter** of this rectangle.

1 mark

2. Find the **area** of the orange shape. Each square is $1\ cm^2$.

1 mark

Challenge 2

PS **1.** Here is a plan of a swimming pool with a blue-tiled border. Each square is $1\ m^2$.

pool

tiled border

a) What is the area of the pool?

b) How can you find the area of the pool **without** counting each square?

c) What is the perimeter of the tiled border?

3 marks

Challenge 3

PS **1.** The perimeter of this shape is 42 cm.

4 cm

3 cm

8 cm

?

9 cm

8 cm 2 cm

4 cm

shape not drawn to scale

Calculate the missing length.

1 mark

Total: /6 marks

Had a go **Getting there** **Got it!**

Measurement

Money

- Convert between different units of measure
- Estimate, compare and calculate different measures, including money in pounds and pence
- Solve simple money problems

Notes and coins

Example

Look at the coins in this purse.
How much money is there in total?
Give your answer as a decimal.

You need to add the value of all the coins together.

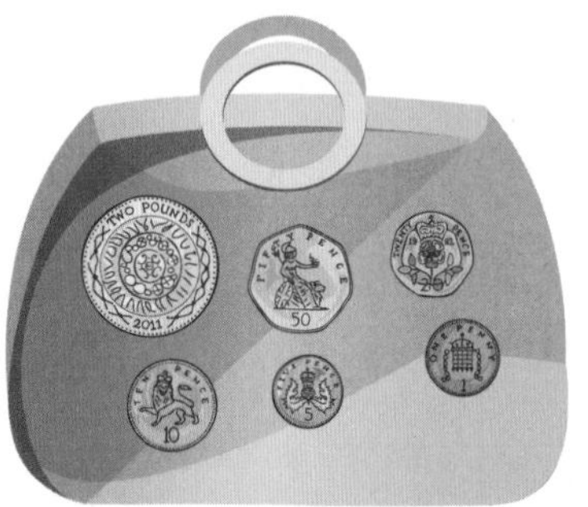

pence (less than £1)

£2.86

whole pounds

£2 + 50p + 20p + 10p + 5p + 1p = £2 and 86p or £2.86

Comparing amounts of money

Example

Which is greater, £6.10 or £6.11?

The number of whole **pounds** is the same in each amount (£6), so we need to look at the value of the **pence**. 11 pence is more than 10 pence.

So, £6.11 is greater than £6.10.

> **Tip**
>
> Always write money with two decimal places. For example: £3 and 10p is £3.10; £3 and 1p is £3.01

Buying shopping

Example

A book costs £3.99 and a comic costs £1.75.

How much **change** do I get from £10, if I buy a comic and a book?

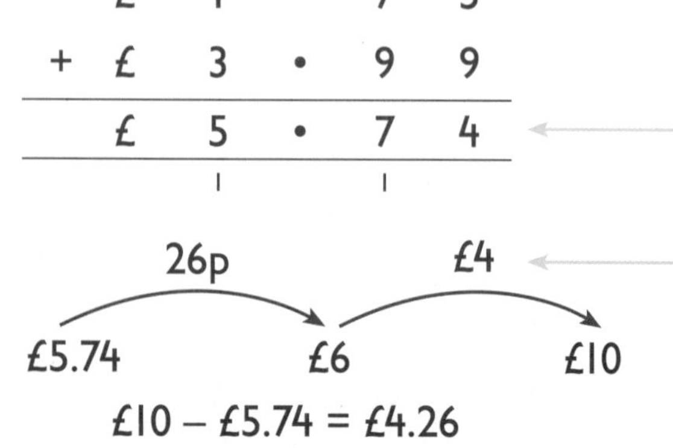

To solve this problem, first we need to find the **total** price of the book and the comic.

Then we calculate the change by subtracting the total from the amount paid. You can do this by finding the difference between the two amounts.

> **Key words**
>
> - pounds (£)
> - pence (p)
> - change
> - total

Challenge 1

1. Write each amount of money as a decimal.

   a) ☐

   b) ☐

   2 marks

2. Write the prices in ascending order.

   a) £4.03 £4.35 £4.53 £4.40 ____________________

   b) £2.90 £9.02 £9.20 £2.99 ____________________

   2 marks

Challenge 2

PS 1. Here are the prices of some items at the café.

£4 and 59p £2 and 75p £3 and 86p £6 and 85p £1 and 55p

   a) What is the cost of a hot dog and an ice-cream? ☐ 1 mark

   b) What is the cost of two bottles of orange juice and a pizza? ☐ 1 mark

   c) Zofia buys an orange juice, a hot dog and an ice-cream. How much change does she get from a £10 note? ☐ 2 marks

Challenge 3

PS 1. Ozi has £15. He wants to use all of his money to buy car models. Each model costs £2.95. What is the maximum number of car models that he can buy? ☐ 1 mark

PS 2. Rosie buys three computer games. Game A costs half as much as Game B.

   Game B costs £30.50. Game C costs twice as much as Game B.

   How much money does Rosie spend in total? ☐ 2 marks

Total: ☐ / 11 marks

Had a go ☐ **Getting there** ☐ **Got it!** ☐

Time

- Read, write and convert time between analogue and digital 12- and 24-hour clocks
- Solve problems involving converting from: hours to minutes; minutes to seconds; years to months; weeks to days

Analogue clocks

An **analogue** clock usually has the numbers 1 to 12 around its face and they split the day into two 12-hour halves. The times from 12 midnight to 12 midday (noon) are **a.m.** times. The times from 12 midday (noon) to 12 midnight are **p.m.** times.

There are two hands on an analogue clock. The shorter hand is the **hour** hand. The longer hand is the **minute** hand.

Tip

The minutes past and minutes to the hour on a clock face are numbers in the 5 times table.

Example

What time is shown on these analogue clocks?

Remember

When you are solving time problems, it important to remember these key **time facts**:

60 **seconds** = 1 minute
60 minutes = 1 hour
24 hours = 1 day
365 days = 1 **year**
366 days = 1 **leap year**
12 **months** = 1 year

Digital clocks

Another type of clock is a **digital** clock. A digital clock displays the time in numbers. Some digital clocks use 12-hour clock times and use a.m. (for morning) and p.m. (for evening). Most digital clocks though, use **24-hour** clock times and use the hours from 00 to 23, so there is no need to use a.m. or p.m.

Example

What time is shown on these digital clocks?

Key words

- analogue
- hour
- minute
- digital
- 24-hour
- second
- year
- leap year
- month

Challenge 1

1. Complete these time fact problems.

a) 2 days = [ ] hours **b)** 3 hours = [ ] minutes

c) $\frac{1}{2}$ year = [ ] months **d)** 48 months = [ ] years

4 marks

2. Write the correct time shown on each analogue clock in **words**.

a)

b)

c)

3 marks

Challenge 2

1. What time do these clocks show? Give your answers in 24-hour digital time.

a) In the morning

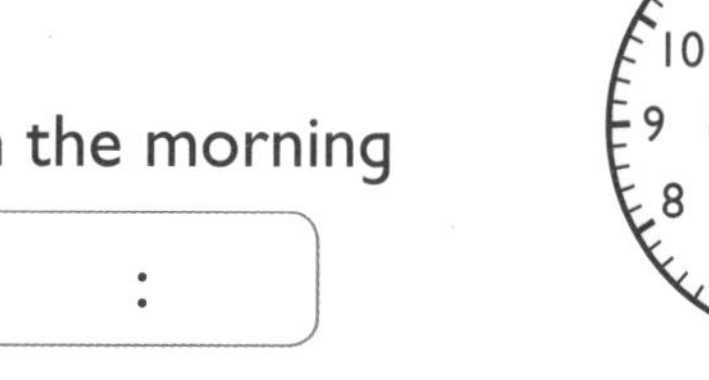

b) In the evening

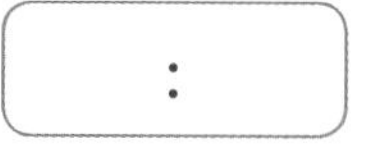

2 marks

PS **2.** Martina puts a whole chicken in the oven at 5:35 p.m. It is ready to take out of the oven at 19:15. How long does the chicken take to roast?

1 mark

Challenge 3

PS **1.** In a school day, 4MQ have 8 lessons that last 40 minutes each. How long does 4MQ spend in lessons each day? Give your answer in hours and minutes.

1 mark

PS **2.** The mini globe cricket tournament happens each leap year. The last tournament was in the summer of 2020. Max says the next tournament will be in 2023.
Do you agree? Explain your answer.

1 mark

Total: [ ] **/ 12 marks**

Had a go [ ] **Getting there** [ ] **Got it!** [ ]

Shapes and lines

- Compare and classify geometric shapes (including quadrilaterals) based on their properties and sizes
- Identify lines of symmetry in 2-D shapes presented in different orientations
- Complete a simple symmetric figure with respect to a specific line of symmetry

Polygons

Polygons are two dimensional (2-D) shapes that have three or more **straight** sides and **vertices**.

Example

Here is a polygon. What is the name of this polygon? Is it a regular or irregular polygon?

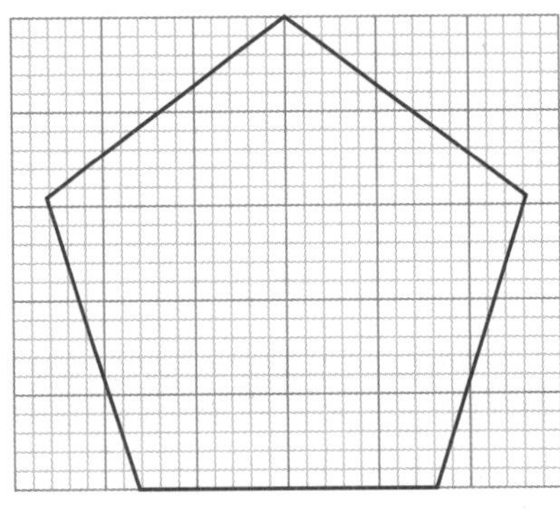

If you count the number of sides and **angles** of the polygon, you will see it has five of each. A polygon that has five straight sides and five angles is called a **pentagon**.

If you look at the pentagon you can see that it has five equal sides and five equal angles, so it is a **regular pentagon**.

This is an example of an **irregular** pentagon:

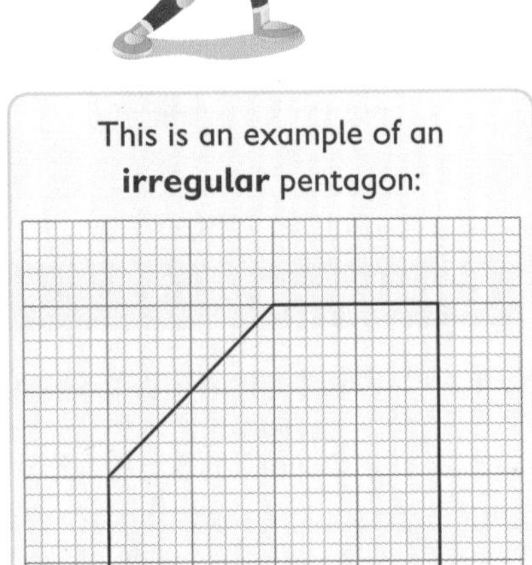

An **irregular** pentagon would not have equal sides or angles.

Quadrilaterals

A **quadrilateral** has four straight sides (**edges**) and four angles.

Example

Describe this quadrilateral.

It is a **trapezium** with one pair of parallel sides.

Symmetry

A 2-D shape is symmetrical if a line can be drawn through it, so that either side of the line looks exactly the same. The line is called a **line of symmetry**.

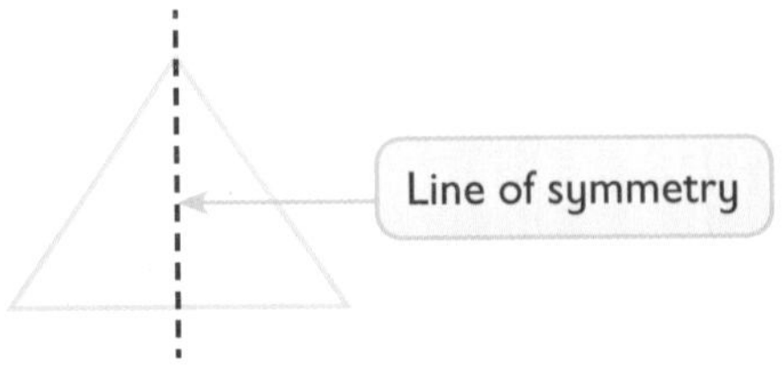

Key words

- polygon
- straight
- vertices
- regular
- irregular
- quadrilateral
- edge

Challenge 1

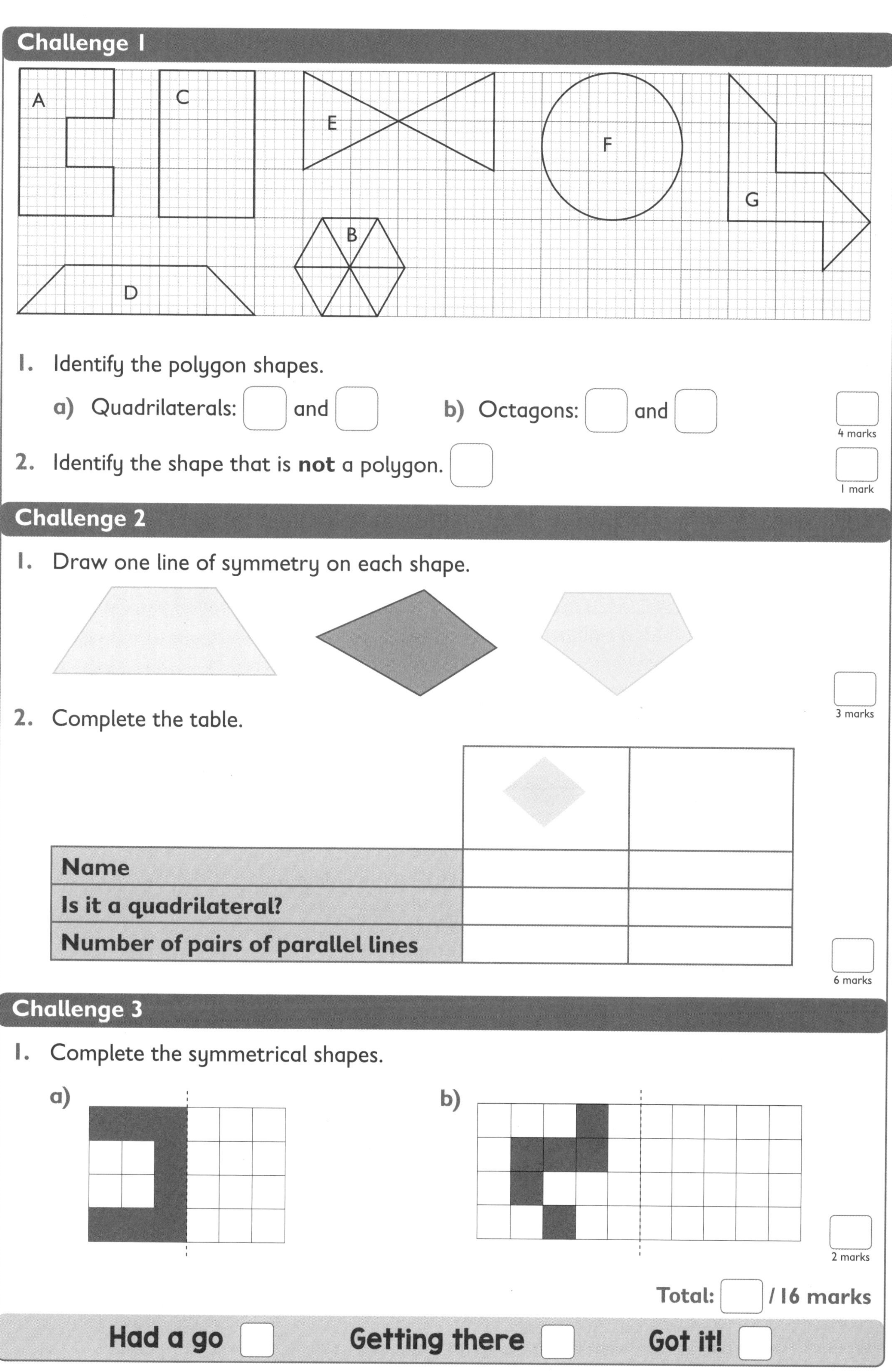

1. Identify the polygon shapes.

   a) Quadrilaterals: ☐ and ☐ b) Octagons: ☐ and ☐

4 marks

2. Identify the shape that is **not** a polygon. ☐

1 mark

Challenge 2

1. Draw one line of symmetry on each shape.

3 marks

2. Complete the table.

Name		
Is it a quadrilateral?		
Number of pairs of parallel lines		

6 marks

Challenge 3

1. Complete the symmetrical shapes.

   a) b)

2 marks

Total: ☐ **/ 16 marks**

Had a go ☐ **Getting there** ☐ **Got it!** ☐

Geometry

Angles and triangles

- Compare and classify geometric shapes (including triangles) based on their properties and sizes
- Identify acute and obtuse angles and compare and order angles up to two right angles by size

What are angles?

An **angle** is the measure of a **turn**. It is formed where two lines meet at a point. Angles are measured in **degrees** (°).

A **right angle** occurs when one straight horizontal line meets a straight vertical line to make a corner. A right angle is equal to 90°, which is the same as a quarter-turn.	
Two right angles are equal to: 90° × 2 = 180°, which is a half-turn.	
An angle that is less than a right angle is called an **acute** angle.	
An angle that is more than one right angle , but less than two right angles, is called an **obtuse** angle.	

Triangles

A **triangle** has three straight sides and three angles. It is a polygon.

You need to be able to recognise different types of triangle: **equilateral**, **isosceles**, **scalene** and **right-angled**.

Equilateral triangle	Isosceles triangle	Scalene triangle	Right-angled triangle
– all the sides are equal – all the angles are 60°	– two of the sides are equal – two of the angles are equal	– all the sides are different lengths – all the angles are different sizes	– one angle is 90°

Key words

- angle
- turn
- degrees (°)
- right angle
- acute
- obtuse
- triangle: equilateral, isosceles, scalene, right-angled

Challenge 1

1. Look at these angles and then complete the sentences.

A B C

a) Angle ☐ is less than a right angle.

b) Angle ☐ is more than a right angle.

c) Angle ☐ is 90 degrees.

3 marks

2. Order these angles from smallest to largest.

A B C D E

____

5 marks

Challenge 2

Here is a square grid. On the grid...

1. Draw and label an isosceles triangle.
2. Draw and label a scalene triangle.
3. Draw and label a right-angled triangle.

3 marks

Challenge 3

1. Dan says the size of the angle between the clock's hands is acute. Do you agree? Explain your answer.

____

____

1 mark

Total: ☐ / 12 marks

Had a go ☐ **Getting there** ☐ **Got it!** ☐

Coordinates and translation

- Describe positions on a 2-D grid as coordinates in the first quadrant
- Describe movements between positions as translations of a given unit to the left/right and up/down
- Plot specified points and draw sides to complete a given polygon

Coordinates

Coordinates are shown on a **coordinate grid**.

Example

Write the coordinate of point A.

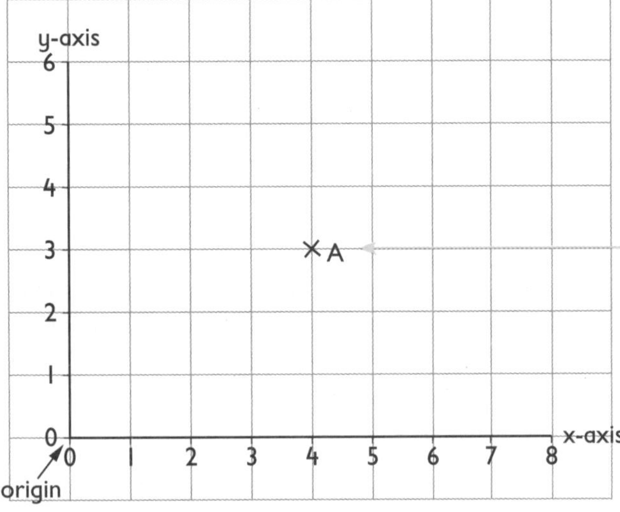

If you read along the x-axis, point A is at the value 4.
Then read up the y-axis and point A is at the value 3.

So, the coordinate for point A is (4,3).

The **horizontal** line is called the **x-axis**.

The **vertical** line is called the **y-axis**.

The **axes** meet at the origin. Both axes are numbered, so you can identify the exact position of a point on the grid.

A **coordinate** is written in brackets, with the x-axis value first and then the y-axis value. A comma is used between the x-axis and y-axis values.

Translation

A **translation** moves a shape *left, right, up* or *down* on a grid. The whole shape moves – it does not change size and still looks the same but is just in a different **position** on the grid.

Example

Describe the translation of shape A to shape B.

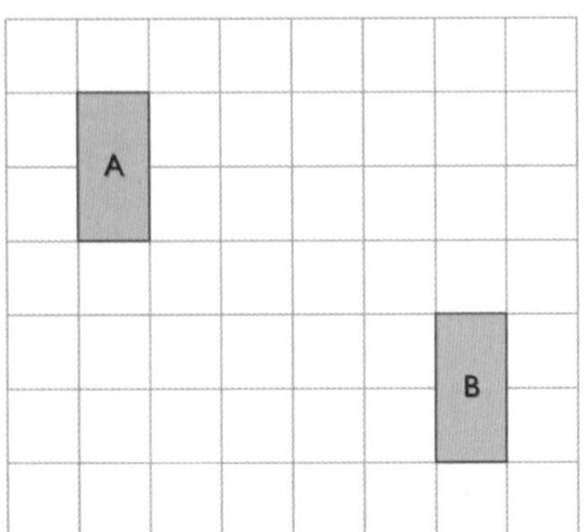

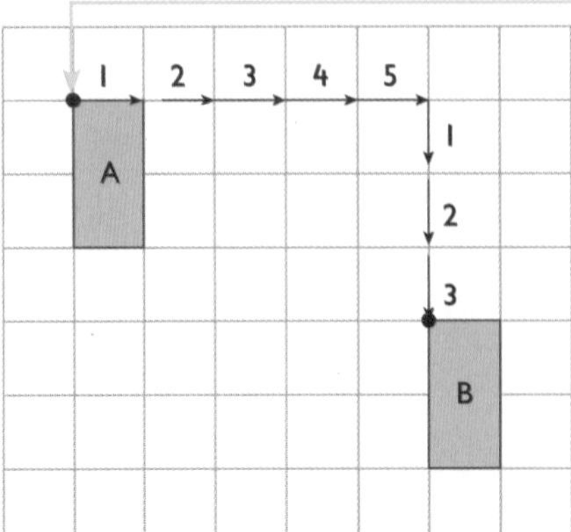

It is helpful to place a dot at one of the corresponding vertices on each shape to count along and describe how the shape has moved.

The translation of shape A to shape B is 5 right, 3 down.

Key words

- coordinates
- coordinate grid
- horizontal
- x-axis
- vertical
- y-axis
- translate
- position

Challenge 1

1. Here is a coordinate grid. Write the coordinate of each point.

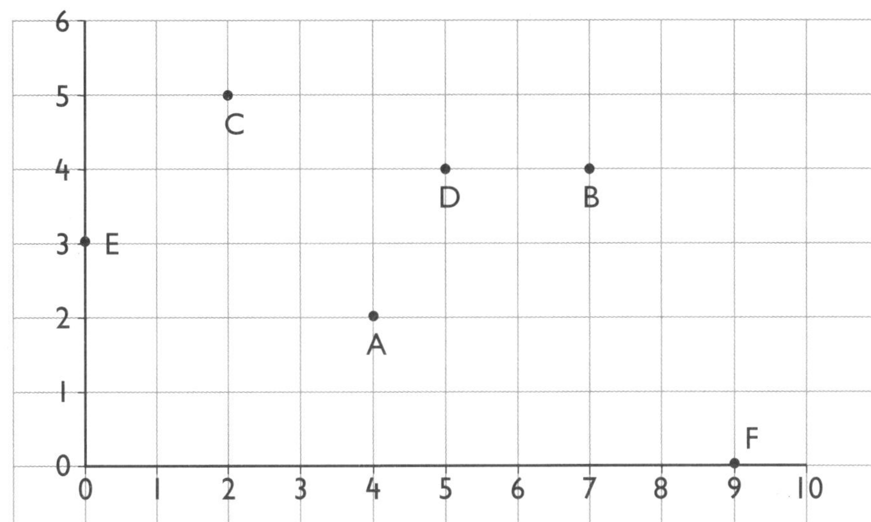

a) A = ☐

b) B = ☐

c) C = ☐

d) D = ☐

e) E = ☐

f) F = ☐

6 marks

Challenge 2

1. Describe the translations.

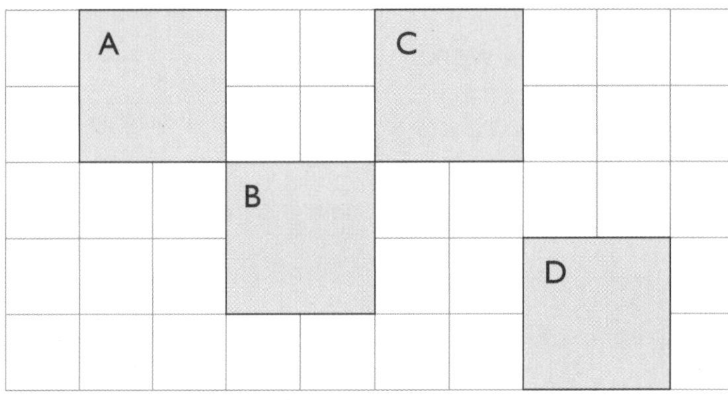

a) A to B ______________

b) D to B ______________

c) B to C ______________

d) D to A ______________

4 marks

Challenge 3

Here is a coordinate grid.

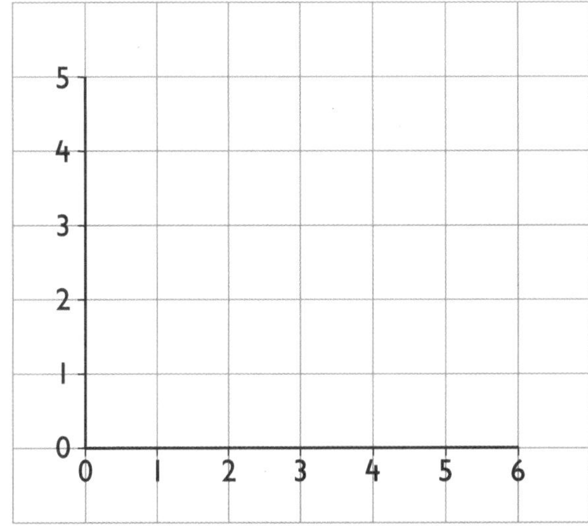

1. Plot these points on the coordinate grid.

   A = (1,2); B = (1,4); C = (2,5);
   D = (5,5); E = (6,4); F = (6,2);
   G = (5,1); H = (2,1).

8 marks

2. Join up all the points from A to H.
   What is the name of the polygon?

   ____

1 mark

Total: ☐ / 19 marks

Had a go ☐ **Getting there** ☐ **Got it!** ☐

Tables and pictograms

- Interpret and present data using pictograms and tables
- Solve one-step and two-step questions using information presented in pictograms and tables

Tables

Tables are used to record information that has been collected. We can use the information in tables to solve one-step and two-step questions, for example, 'How many more...?' and 'How many fewer...?'.

Information can be recorded in a **frequency** table. The word frequency means how often something happens. A frequency table is made using a **tally**. A tally is when you make a mark each time you collect a piece of information.

Tip

You make a tally by first making four vertical marks and then drawing the next mark through the first four, to make a 'gate' of five marks.

Example

Looking at the frequency table, how many more ants were found than beetles?

Mini beast	Tally	Frequency
Ladybird	卌 III	8
Beetle	卌 卌 II	12
Ant	卌 卌 卌 卌 IIII	24
Spider	卌 I	6
Snail	卌 III	8

You need to look at the table carefully. There are 12 beetles and 24 ants.
$24 - 12 = 12$.

So, 12 more ants were found than beetles.

Pictograms

A **pictogram** uses simple pictures or **symbols** to represent one or more pieces of data.

Example

This pictogram shows the number of people who played tennis over the weekend on Court B. How many people played tennis on Saturday?

Number of people playing tennis on Court B	
Saturday	
Sunday	

(symbol) = 10 people

You need to add the symbols together. Each whole symbol is equal to 10 people.

For Saturday, there are 4 whole symbols plus a $\frac{1}{2}$ symbol.

4×10 people = 40 people; $\frac{1}{2}$ of a whole symbol = 5 people

So, $40 + 5 = 45$ people.

Key words

- table
- frequency
- tally
- pictogram
- symbol

Challenge 1

1. Here is a chart showing the food that five children like.

	Pizza	Pasta	Roast dinner	Burgers	Tofu
Arya	★	★			
Harry		★	★		
Scott	★	★	★		
Kamal			★		
Katie		★			★

a) Which food is the most popular?

____

b) Who likes tofu?

____

c) Who does not like pasta?

____

3 marks

Challenge 2

1. This pictogram shows the number of pizzas sold by each pizza restaurant.

Pizza2Go	
PizzaHot	
Fast Pizza	
Cheesy Pizza	

= 6 pizzas

a) How many pizzas did *PizzaHot* sell?

b) Mel says *Pizza2Go* sold 3½ pizzas. Do you agree? Explain your answer.

____

c) How many more pizzas did *Fast Pizza* sell than *Cheesy Pizza*?

3 marks

Challenge 3

1. This table and pictogram shows the number of letters received during one week.

Day	Number of letters
Monday	800
Tuesday	700
Wednesday	500
Thursday	1,000

Monday	
Tuesday	
Wednesday	
Thursday	

= ?

a) How many letters does each symbol represent?

b) Complete the symbols for Thursday.

2 marks

Total: /8 marks

Had a go **Getting there** **Got it!**

Bar charts

- Interpret and present data using bar charts and time graphs
- Solve one-step and two-step questions using information presented in bar charts and time graphs

Bar charts

Bar charts are another way to show **data**. They are very useful for comparing two or more groups of data.

For example: The bar charts on the right show Sam's test scores. Bar chart A shows the data using **vertical** bars. Bar chart B shows the data using **horizontal** bars. They show the same information. The height or length of the bars tells you the score.

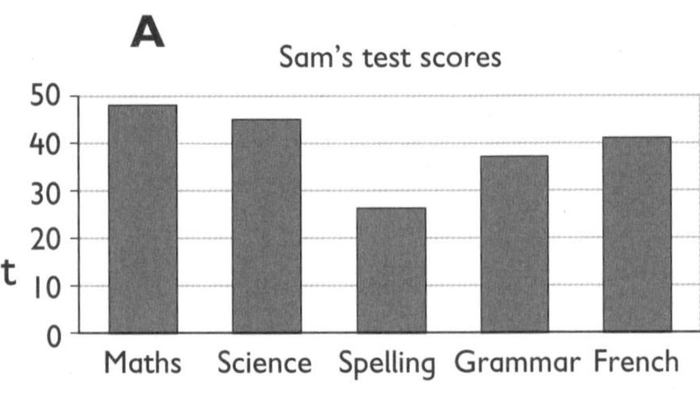

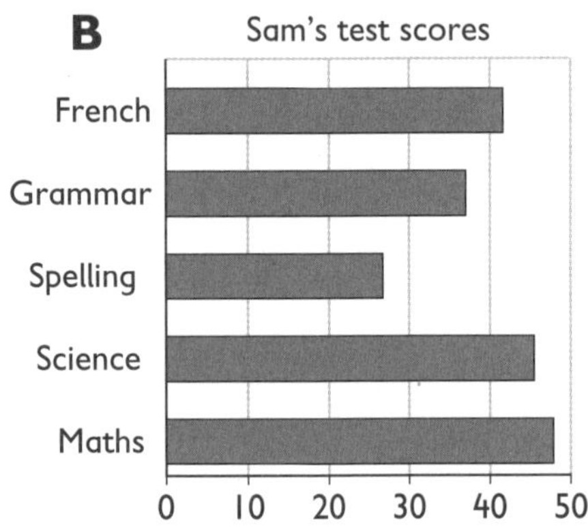

Example

Look at bar charts A and B. In which subject did Sam score less than 30 marks?

For bar chart A, you need to go up the **y-axis** to 30 and then look for any subject where the bar is below the 30-mark score level. For bar chart B, you need to go along the **x-axis** to 30 and look for any subject that is shorter than the 30-mark score line.

So, the subject that Sam scored less than 30 marks in is Spelling.

> **Tip**
>
> You must look carefully at the scale on each axis.

Time graphs

Information collected over a period of time, such as temperature or distance from a certain place, can be displayed as a **time graph**.

Example

How many days did it take for the plant to grow to 70 cm?

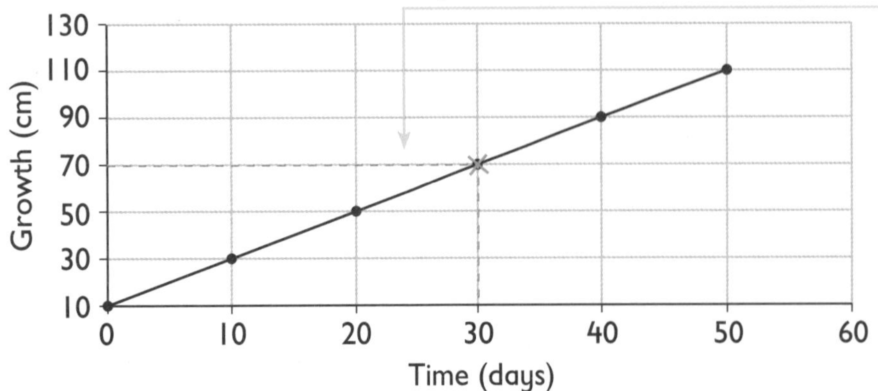

You need to interpret the graph by reading up the y-axis (growth) to 70 cm – go across the graph to draw a cross on the line and read straight down from the cross to the x-axis (time) to find the number of days.

So, it took 30 days for the sunflower plant to grow to 70 cm.

> **Key words**
>
> - bar chart
> - data
> - vertical
> - horizontal
> - y-axis
> - x-axis
> - time graph

Challenge 1

1. This bar chart shows the maths test scores of five children.

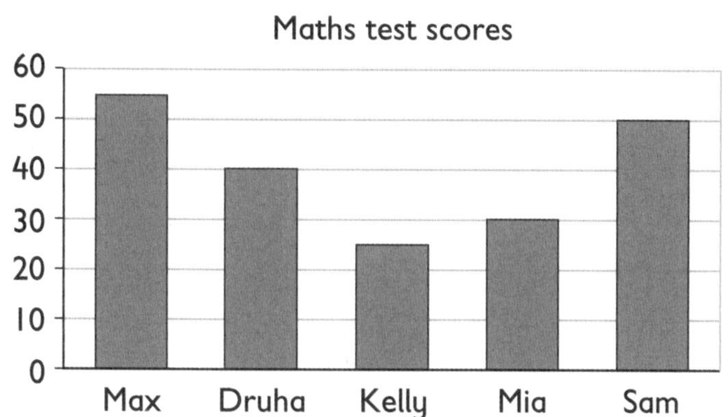

a) Who had the highest score on the maths test? ____________

b) What was the difference between Druha and Sam's score? [ ]

2 marks

Challenge 2

1. This graph shows the growth of a seed to a young plant.

Graph showing the growth of a seed to a plant

Height (cm): 0, 2, 4, 6, 8, 10, 12, 14, 16, 18

Number (days): 0, 2, 4, 6, 8, 10

a) On what day was the plant 14 cm tall? ____________

b) How tall was the plant on day 4? [ ] cm

c) How much did the plant grow between day 3 and day 8? [ ] cm

3 marks

Challenge 3

Look at this graph of a delivery driver's journey.

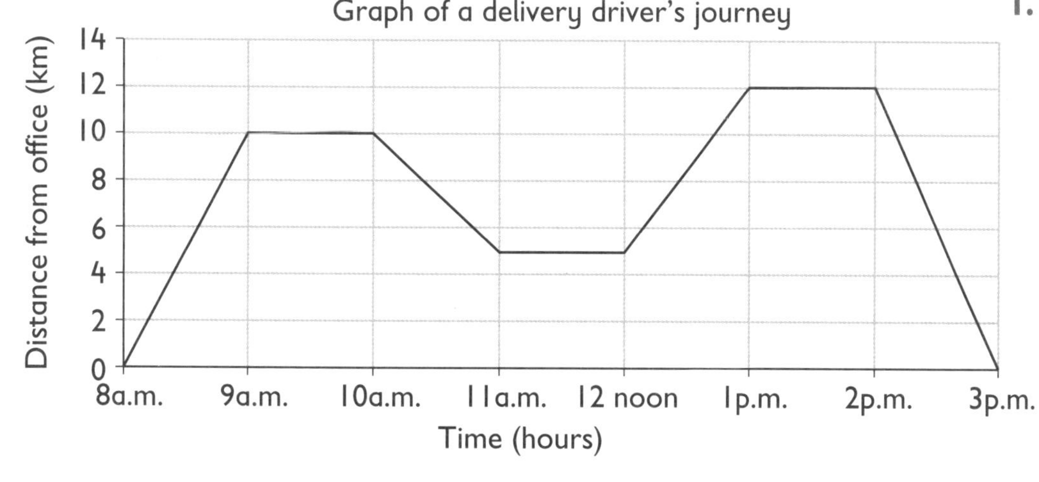

1. Write the times of the day when the delivery driver is loading his van with packages.

____

____

____

1 mark

Total: [ ] /6 marks

Had a go [ ] **Getting there** [ ] **Got it!** [ ]

Progress test 4

1. **Complete the sequences.**

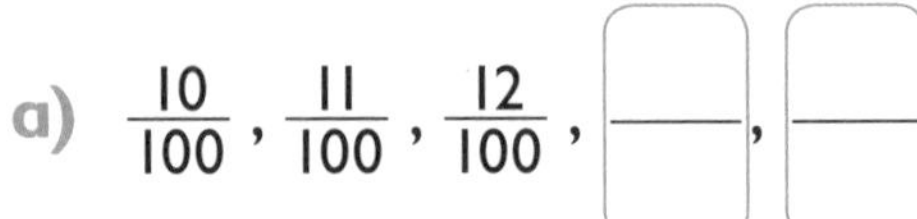

a) $\frac{10}{100}$, $\frac{11}{100}$, $\frac{12}{100}$, $\frac{\square}{\square}$, $\frac{\square}{\square}$

b) 0.2, 0.3, 0.4, ☐, ☐

2 marks

2. **Here is a pattern made of square tiles. Each tile is 1 m^2.**

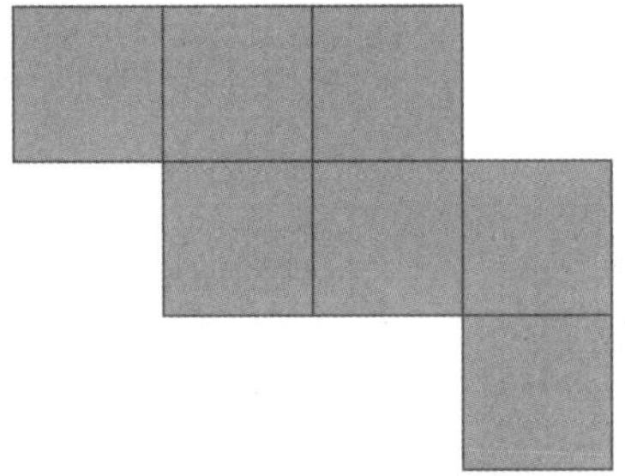

What is the area of the pattern? ☐

1 mark

PS 3. **Four friends share 36p equally. How much do they each get?** ☐

1 mark

4. **Write in digits the number 'five hundred and seven'.** ☐

1 mark

5. **Complete the boxes.**

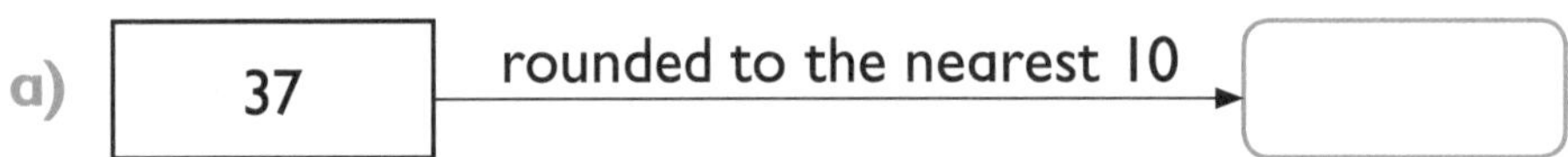

a) 37 → rounded to the nearest 10 → ☐

b) 188 → rounded to the nearest 10 → ☐

c) 253 → rounded to the nearest 100 → ☐

3 marks

PS 6. **Ryan has £467. Sally has £1,000 more than Ryan.**

How much does Sally have? £ ☐

1 mark

7. **Complete the calculations.**

a)

	Th	H	T	O
	4	5	8	6
+	1	2	1	4

b)

	Th	H	T	O
	8	9	5	5
−	5	3	8	1

2 marks

8. Here are six numbers.

4,508 4,681 4,590 4,399 4,182 4,903

Write the numbers in **descending** order.

____

1 mark

PS **9. Complete the fraction sentences.**

a) $\frac{1}{5} = \frac{\square}{10} = \frac{\square}{20}$

b) $\frac{\square}{2} = \frac{3}{6} = \frac{\square}{8}$

4 marks

10. Tick the statement that is equal to 288.

9 × 4 × 8 ☐ **3 × 6 × 6** ☐ **6 × 6 × 6** ☐

1 mark

PS **11. Here is an ice-cream menu.**

Cone:	1 scoop	£2.80	2 scoops	£3.25
Cup:	1 scoop	£1.95	2 scoops	£2.35

a) Sidra buys a cone with 1 scoop and a cup with 2 scoops. How much does he pay in total? £ ☐

b) Anika pays for a cone with 2 scoops and a cup with 1 scoop using a £10 note. How much change does she get in total? £ ☐

2 marks

12. Match each fraction to the equivalent decimal.

$\frac{1}{2}$ $\frac{1}{5}$ $\frac{3}{4}$ $\frac{1}{100}$

0.75 0.2 0.5 0.01

4 marks

PS **13. There are 30 sheets of stickers in a pack.**

Each sheet has the same number of stickers. There are 360 stickers altogether in a pack.

How many stickers are on each sheet? ☐

1 mark

14. Complete the fraction calculations.

a) $\frac{3}{10} + \frac{8}{10} = \frac{\square}{\square}$

b) $\frac{2}{12} + \frac{\square}{\square} = \frac{10}{12}$

c) $\frac{45}{100} - \frac{20}{100} = \frac{\square}{\square}$

3 marks

PS **15. Jane makes a 4-digit number using the numbers in the oval shapes.**

1,000 1,000
1,000 100
1 10
100

Write this number in words.

____

____

1 mark

PS **16. Sort these shapes into groups by putting the letter of each shape into the correct box in the table.**

A 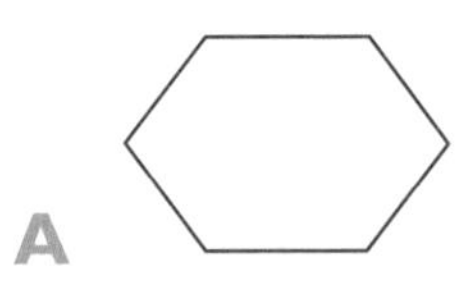 B C 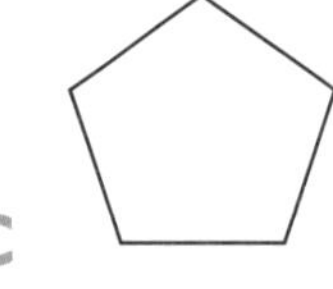 D 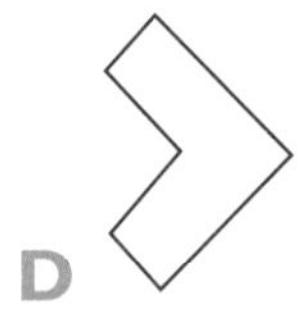 E 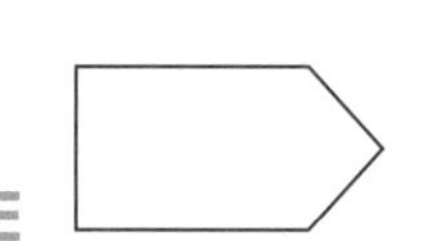 F

	Regular	**Not regular**
Quadrilateral		
Not a quadrilateral		

6 marks

PS **17. A box of chocolates contains dark, milk and white chocolates.**

$\frac{5}{12}$ of the box are milk chocolates. $\frac{1}{3}$ of the box are white chocolates.

What fraction of the box are dark chocolates? $\frac{\square}{\square}$

1 mark

PS 18. This is a smoothie recipe for 10 people. Change the recipe so it is correct for 1 person.

Recipe for 10 people
600 g berries
500 ml milk
250 g of yoghurt
35 g of sugar

Recipe for 1 person
________ g berries
________ ml milk
________ g of yoghurt
________ g of sugar

4 marks

19. Here are four angles.

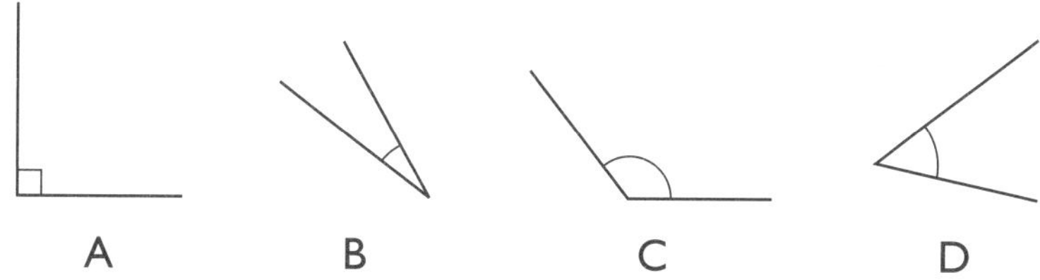

a) Order the angles from smallest to largest. ______ ______ ______ ______

1 mark

b) Use these words to complete the sentence.

acute **obtuse** **right**

Angle A is a ________ angle.

Angle B is an ________ angle.

Angle C is an ________ angle.

3 marks

20. Year 4 are collecting marbles. They have 57 marbles in total.

Complete the bar for the number of yellow marbles.

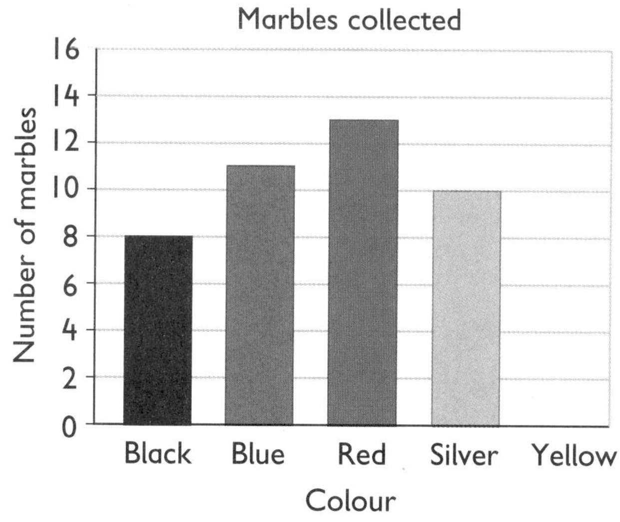

1 mark

Total: ____ /44 marks

Writing – Vocabulary, grammar and punctuation

Sentences

- Extend the use of sentences with more than one clause
- Understand the role of the determiner

Using different clauses

A clause is part of a sentence and contains a subject and a verb.

Example

Sentences can have one or more clauses.

Example

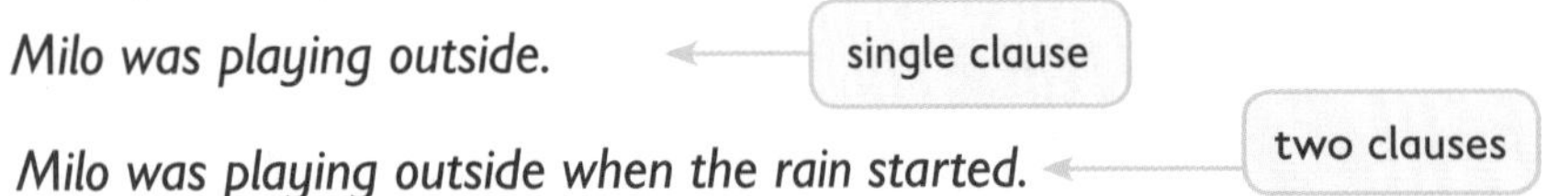

Sentences become more detailed and more interesting when they have more than one clause. Different clauses are joined with **conjunctions**.

Example

and → *We went to the shop* ***and*** *we went to the cinema.*
or → *They usually go swimming* ***or*** *walking on a Saturday.*
but → *We like going walking* ***but*** *we prefer to go swimming.*
when → *They do not go walking* ***when*** *they go swimming.*
if → *There is not time for swimming* ***if*** *they go walking.*
because → *They cannot go swimming* ***because*** *they go walking.*
although → *They went walking* ***although*** *they wished they had gone swimming.*

Determiners

Determiners give more information about a noun, e.g. **a** and **the** are determiners.

Example

a *flying bird*		***a*** *young girl*	could refer to any flying bird or young girl
my *flying bird*		***your*** *flying bird*	refers to a particular bird or girl
the *girl*	***that*** *girl*	***this*** *girl*	

Remember

The determiner can help give the noun more clarity, often by being more specific.

Tip

Check that the sentence has the intended meaning when a conjunction has been written.

Remember

Determiners can also be used for quantities, e.g.
- every flying bird
- some girls

Key words

- conjunction
- determiner

Challenge 1

1. Read each sentence. Underline the conjunction and circle the determiner(s).

   a) They had a great time when they went to the circus.

   b) School will open if we can clear this snow.

   c) Everyone jumped when Bruce dropped his pan.

   d) We washed our hands and then went for our lunch.

   e) We had a new teacher today because Mr White was ill.

10 marks

Challenge 2

1. Draw a line to join up the two parts of each sentence.

a) There will be a big celebration if	I am full.
b) You can have the cake because	I prefer honey.
c) We will be happy when	the team wins today.
d) I like jam although	the journey is over.

4 marks

Challenge 3

1. Add a conjunction so each sentence makes sense.

   a) Eli was happy ____________ his mum found his lost teddy.

   b) ____________ they get one more point, they will win the prize.

   c) You will need your coat ____________ it will get cold later.

   d) ____________ we have had a story, it will be time to go home.

4 marks

2. Create a sentence about your school using each given conjunction.

   a) but ____

   b) although ____

   c) when ____

   d) if ____

4 marks

Total: ☐ / 22 marks

Had a go ☐ **Getting there** ☐ **Got it!** ☐

Fronted adverbials

- Use fronted adverbials to enhance sentence structure and description

Adverbials

An **adverbial** is a word, phrase or clause that is used like an adverb to add extra information to a verb.

Example

They ate their lunch in a posh restaurant.

adverbial phrase

Leo hopped all the way to school.

The adverbial phrase in each sentence is giving more details about the eating of lunch and Leo hopping.

Remember

It is important to vary sentence structure and give the reader additional detail.

Starting a sentence with an adverbial

Adverbials at the start of a sentence are known as **fronted adverbials**.
They describe the action that will follow in the sentence.

Example

All the way to school, Leo hopped.

The adverbial phrase is at the beginning of the sentence.

In a posh restaurant, they ate their lunch.

The fronted adverbial can also indicate time.

Example

Before we went on holiday, *we packed our cases.*
After the final song, *everybody applauded and cheered.*
During the storm, *we hid under the stairs.*

Fronted adverbials not only provide additional information and description, but also add variety to the sentence openers being used in a piece of writing. They help to engage the reader by making the text more interesting.

Tip

Many fronted adverbials should be followed by a comma. The best bet is to add a comma if you are unsure.

Key words

- adverbial
- fronted adverbial

Challenge 1

1. Underline the fronted adverbial in each sentence.

   a) After the game, the team lifted the trophy.

   b) Under the bed, she found an old newspaper.

   c) Later, there will be free sweets at the disco.

   d) Originally, they had planned to walk to school.

4 marks

Challenge 2

1. Match each fronted adverbial to the best sentence ending.

a) In the ghost train ride,	he saw a jellyfish.
b) At the cinema,	I saw some creepy creatures.
c) When Dad was in the water,	we watched a great film.

3 marks

Challenge 3

1. Rewrite each sentence so that the adverbial phrase becomes a fronted adverbial.

   a) We went to the shops after lunch.

   ____

   b) We saw whales when we were on the ferry.

   ____

   c) I got some fish and chips on the way home.

   ____

   d) It rained straight after our football match.

   ____

   e) You need your coat on before you go outside.

   ____

5 marks

Total: ☐ / 12 marks

Had a go ☐ Getting there ☐ Got it! ☐

Noun phrases

- Expand noun phrases by using modifying adjectives, nouns and preposition phrases

Modifying adjectives

An **expanded noun phrase** has a noun or pronoun, and words that describe the noun or pronoun (adjectives).

Example

a kind, friendly person

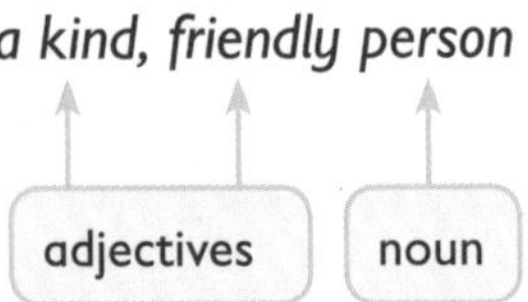

Remember

A noun is a person, place or thing. A pronoun is a word used to replace a noun, e.g. he, she, it, they

Providing more detail makes the writing more interesting. The phrase 'kind, friendly person' is more interesting than saying 'a person'. In this example, the adjectives modify the noun – they give more detail about the person.

Tip

Think of interesting adjectives e.g. try 'wonderful' instead of 'nice' and 'huge' instead of big.

Modifying nouns

A noun can be used to modify another noun that follows it.

Example

Penny wore a summer dress.

the noun **summer** describes the particular dress she wore

They all had a cup of blackcurrant juice.

the noun **blackcurrant** describes the juice

Prepositional phrases

Prepositional phrases modify the noun phrase by telling us more about place or time.

Example

Penny wore a summer dress ***all year round****.*

Garth is a gentleman ***in our village****.*

They all had a cup of juice ***at the café.***

Key word

- expanded noun phrase

Challenge 1

1. Match pairs of nouns that work together as a noun phrase.

school	fire
bathroom	court
log	door
train	field
tennis	station

5 marks

Challenge 2

1. Underline the expanded noun phrase in each sentence.

   a) There was a hat on the empty chair.

   b) It was a red, felt hat.

   c) My cousin has an amazing guitar.

   d) We like the food in the new café in town.

4 marks

Challenge 3

1. Add a prepositional phrase to complete each sentence.

   a) Jack's new, red football went ______________________________.

   b) The beautiful village is ______________________________.

   c) A fine, cool drizzle fell ______________________________.

   d) The speeding train travelled ______________________________.

4 marks

2. Add a modifying noun to each sentence.

   a) The children gave their mum a ______________ bracelet.

   b) In the supermarket, Sam took out his ______________ list.

   c) The crowd were singing at the ______________ match.

   d) They used the ______________ scales to weigh the flour.

4 marks

Total: ☐ / 17 marks

Had a go ☐ Getting there ☐ Got it! ☐

Direct speech

- Use inverted commas and other punctuation to indicate direct speech

Direct speech

Direct speech is used in writing to show the exact words a character says.

Example

Both sentences below are about the same thing.

"It is time for tea now," said Sam.

Sam told them that it was time for tea.

The direct speech tells us the exact words that Sam said are **It is time for tea now.**

Remember

Speaking characters help bring a text to life, but the speech needs careful punctuation.

Punctuating direct speech

Direct speech is punctuated using **inverted commas**. They are placed around the spoken words. Additional punctuation is also needed.

Example

"It is time for tea now."

The words **said Sam**, although not spoken, still need adding to the sentence to show who spoke.

"It is time for tea now," said Sam.

The sentence is punctuated with a **comma** after the final spoken word, before the second inverted commas. The sentence also needs a full stop at the end.

Sometimes, the information about who said the words is given before the words themselves.

Example

Sam said, "It is time for tea now."

A comma usually follows the words telling us who spoke. Each time inverted commas are used, the first spoken word always has a capital letter.

Tip

If the spoken words are a question or exclamation, the correct punctuation mark is used instead of a comma.

Key words

- direct speech
- inverted commas
- comma

Challenge 1

1. Rewrite these sentences, adding in the inverted commas.

   a) This is a lovely picture, said Mr Harb.

   ____

   b) Let's get going, urged Dad.

   ____

   c) What time is the last train? asked the lady.

   ____

3 marks

Challenge 2

1. Rewrite these examples of direct speech, adding the missing punctuation.

   a) The taxi is here said Ella.

   ____

   b) Sophie said Look at how busy the beach is.

   ____

   c) What would you like to drink asked the waiter.

   ____

   d) Connie asked, Who would like to play with me?

   ____

4 marks

Challenge 3

1. Turn each of the sentences below into direct speech.

   a) Abbie said to her brother that he could not play.

   ____

   b) Carlo asked his sister for help with his homework.

   ____

   c) Joe told his cousin he would see her soon.

   ____

3 marks

Total: ☐ / 10 marks

Had a go ☐ **Getting there ☐** **Got it! ☐**

Nouns and pronouns

- Choose pronouns and nouns appropriately to avoid repetition

Replacing nouns with pronouns

If a **noun** is repeated too many times, writing becomes less interesting to read.

Example

The boat was blue. Tom got in the boat. Slowly Tom rowed the boat across the lake.

The noun **boat** is repeated too often so it needs replacing.

Pronouns are used in place of nouns to avoid repeating the same word all the time.

Example

*The boat was blue. Tom got in **it**. Slowly **he** rowed **it** across the lake.*

The pronoun **it** replaces the word **boat** – the reader knows that **it** means **boat** in each sentence. The proper noun **Tom** is also replaced with the pronoun **he**.

Pronouns should be used to replace names as well as objects. There is no rule for how many times a pronoun should be used, but there should be a good variety of the noun and pronoun to make the writing interesting and easier to read.

Example

*Zara reached the top of the hill. **It** was high and **she** could see for miles. **She** had always wanted to climb **it**. This hill was beautiful and Zara had realised her ambition.*

Both 'the hill' and 'Zara' are used twice, but other mentions are replaced with pronouns. 'hill' is replaced with **it** twice, and 'Zara' is replaced with **she** twice.

It is important to use the correct pronoun.

personal pronouns	possessive pronouns
I, me	mine
they, them	theirs
he, him	his
she, her	hers
it	its
we, us	ours
you	yours

Remember

A noun is the name given to an object. A pronoun replaces a noun.

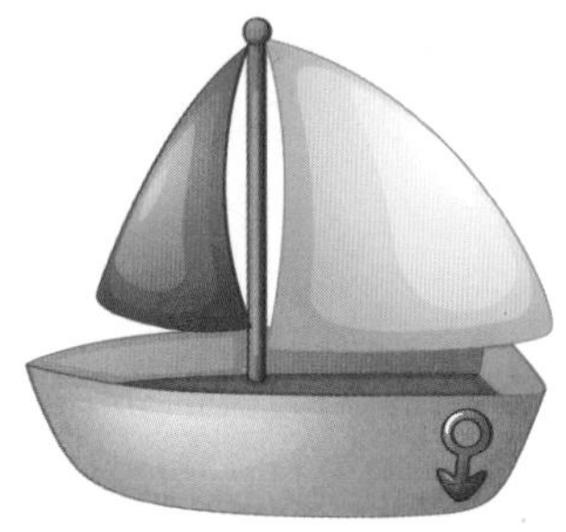

Tip

Make sure it is clear to the reader what the relevant noun is before using pronouns.

Key words

- noun
- pronoun

Challenge 1

1. Underline the personal pronoun in each sentence.

   a) Suzy ate the bread because she was hungry.

   b) Daisy had to walk to school when she moved house.

   c) Luke and Amy were lost and they began to cry.

   d) The creature stared and it looked fierce.

4 marks

Challenge 2

1. Add the correct possessive pronoun into each sentence.

   a) Sunita used my bike because ________ was broken.

   b) We found the creature and now it is ________.

   c) I saw you next to the sports car but I knew it was not ________.

   d) My brother gave me a toy car even better than ________.

4 marks

Challenge 3

1. Rewrite the passage below, replacing the words in bold with suitable pronouns.

Stan went to **Stan's** den. **Stan** stayed in **the den** for hours. It was lunchtime when **Stan** appeared. Stan asked **Stan's mum** what was for lunch. **Stan's mum** asked **Stan** what **Stan** would like for **Stan's** lunch.

____

____

____

____

____

9 marks

Total: ☐ / 17 marks

Had a go ☐ Getting there ☐ Got it! ☐

Apostrophes

- **Use apostrophes to indicate singular and plural possession**

Possessive apostrophes

The **possessive apostrophe** is used to show ownership. If a cake belongs to Noah, or a ball belongs to Isla, or a bone belongs to the dog, an apostrophe is used when stating this ownership. There are two rules for using **apostrophes**.

Rule 1

For words that do not end in **s**, add an apostrophe then add **s** (**'s**).

Example

Noah's cake

Isla's ball

the dog's bone

The word showing the name of the owner does not end in **s** so **'s** is added.

Rule 2

For words already ending in **s**, an apostrophe is written after the s (**s'**).

Example

the bus' driver
bus already ends in **s** so the apostrophe is added after the **s**.

Gus' pen
for names ending in **s**, just add an apostrophe after the **s**.

the twins' birthday
twins is a plural word. For plurals ending in **s**, add the apostrophe after the **s**.

Remember

Apostrophes are also used for contractions of words such as **do not** (don't) and **we are** (we're).

Tip

Be careful with **it's** and **its**. An apostrophe is only used in **it's** when showing a contraction but not for possession. (Contraction: it is = it's, e.g. It's hot today. Possession: only uses its, e.g. The dog lost its ball.)

Key words

- possessive apostrophe
- apostrophe

Challenge 1

1. Copy each word underlined below and add the apostrophe correctly.

   a) the ships captain ______________________

   b) Franks computer ______________________

   c) the old mans photograph ______________________

   d) James bike ______________________

4 marks

Challenge 2

1. Circle the correct word to show possession in each sentence.

   a) We saw **Evie's / Evies'** pets.

   b) The **dog's / dogs** ball was yellow.

   c) The cat scratched **its / it's** owner.

   d) In assembly they said the **girls / girls'** team had won again.

4 marks

Challenge 3

1. Write a sentence that uses a possessive apostrophe for each idea below.

   a) a cat belonging to the girl

   ____

   b) a wheel belonging to the bus

   ____

   c) a toy belonging to Ross

   ____

   d) a book belonging to Mia

   ____

   e) a football belonging to the boys

   ____

5 marks

Total: ☐ / 13 marks

Had a go ☐ **Getting there** ☐ **Got it!** ☐

Progress test 5

1. Read the text below.

They borded the boat as the sun started to set and heded out to see. All was calm and they soon lowerd the fishing nets. Before midnight they had plenty of fish and decided to head home By now the sea was getting rough as a strong wind blew into them. rain started and they culd no longer see the lights from the shore. The boat was tosed up and down for several hours.

a) Proofread the text and circle each of the spelling and punctuation errors.

8 marks

b) Rewrite the first and last sentences, starting them with the given words.

First sentence: As... ______________________________

____

Last sentence: For... ______________________________

____

2 marks

2. Here is a plan for a piece of writing about buying a dog. Think of a suitable name for each subheading.

Subheading	Paragraph
a) ______________________	Paragraph 1 – Different types Paragraph 2 – Which is best for me? Paragraph 3 – Where to buy them.
b) ______________________	Paragraph 1 – Feeding a dog. Paragraph 2 – Giving a dog exercise.

2 marks

3. **Add the suffix -ation to each verb and then explain what the new noun means.**

a) prepare ________________

____

b) adore ________________

____

c) imagine ________________

____

3 marks

4. **Draw a line to join up the two parts of each sentence.**

a) Your lunch will be ready when	it is healthy.
b) I have made some biscuits although	you eat your soup.
c) You can try them if	they look a little hard.
d) You must eat your soup because	you have got changed.

4 marks

5. **Rewrite and change each sentence so that the adverbial phrase or clause becomes a fronted adverbial.**

a) There was a rainbow after the rain.

____

b) Jack jumped when he saw the clown.

____

c) I hurt my leg when I fell over.

____

d) It was a lovely day before it got so windy.

____

4 marks

6. **Add a prepositional phrase to complete each sentence.**

a) Sophie's lovely shoes were ________________________.

b) A large, blue ship sailed ________________________.

c) The cold, wet snow lay ________________________.

3 marks

7. **Add the correct possessive pronoun into each sentence.**

a) Fred's dog is brown so I know the black one is not ____________.

b) If you win, the prize is ____________ to keep.

c) They had a few metres to the finish line where glory would be ____________.

d) This is my sister's room and everything in it is ____________.

4 marks

8. **Copy each word underlined below and add the apostrophe correctly.**

a) the <u>bees</u> hive ____________________

b) <u>Ellas</u> new scooter ____________________

c) the <u>ladies</u> changing room ____________________

d) the <u>hotels</u> reception ____________________

4 marks

9. **Rewrite the passage below, replacing the words in bold with suitable pronouns.**

Mum went to **Mum's** work because **Mum** had left her phone behind. **Mum's** phone was where **Mum** had left **Mum's phone** on **Mum's** desk. Mum's desk was very tidy. **Mum's desk** looked like **Mum's desk** had been cleaned by the cleaners. **The cleaners** were very kind.

____

____

____

____

9 marks

10. **Match each pair of nouns that work together as a noun phrase.**

church | garden | water | star | fish

shed | tank | bells | jug | prize

5 marks

11. Read the poem and then answer the questions.

Storm
The sun slides away,
Behind towering, dark clouds.
A stiff breeze arrives,
Blowing dry sand.
The calm sea slowly starts to rage,
And angry waves crash onto the beach.
The heavens boom and flash,
As the storm arrives.

a) What does the word 'towering' tell the reader about the clouds?

____

b) What does the line 'The calm sea slowly starts to rage' mean?

____

c) How are the waves described?

____

d) What does 'The heavens boom and flash' tell the reader about the storm?

____

4 marks

12. Write each word of French origin in the correct sentence.

technique **fatigue** **unique** **colleague**

a) The model was the only one of its kind – it was ______________.

b) My mum gave her ______________ a lift to work.

c) After running for several hours, ______________ set in.

d) The art teacher showed them a new ______________ for painting.

4 marks

Total: /56 marks

English mixed questions

1. Match each fronted adverbial to the best sentence ending.

a) At the roadside,	some people were fishing.
b) During the winter,	we had a quick snack.
c) Next to the river,	everyone was full.
d) After the meal,	we saw a police car.
e) A few minutes ago,	we wrap up warm.

5 marks

2. Underline the expanded noun phrase in each sentence.

a) A fish lived under the deep blue sea.

b) It was a green, spotty fish.

c) The fish hid under large rocks.

d) It likes to be away from the nipping crabs.

e) There was a large, vicious crab.

5 marks

3. Rewrite and change each of the sentences below into direct speech.

a) The teacher told them to work on their own.

____

b) James asked his mum if she wanted help with lunch.

____

c) Elsa said that she was going on holiday.

____

d) Simone asked when they would be getting home.

____

4 marks

4. Circle the word in each sentence that uses the possessive apostrophe correctly.

a) Yesterday **Sams' / Sam's** cat caught a mouse.

b) **Bess' / Besss** house is across the road from mine.

c) The car was dumped there and we don't know **its / it's** owner.

d) **Mack's / Macks'** pet spider has escaped.

4 marks

5. Add a possessive pronoun into each sentence correctly.

a) Share my lunch because you forgot ________.

b) He came to our school after ________ old school closed.

c) I have to go for tea because my parents are eating ________.

d) We will let you take that taxi because ________ is on its way.

4 marks

6. Rewrite each sentence so that the adverbial phrase becomes a fronted adverbial.

a) The boat arrived as we got there.

____

b) There were lots of parties when we had our fifth birthdays.

____

c) Dan did a crazy dance when he heard his team had won.

____

d) Only two people went outside when it was really cold.

____

4 marks

7. **Read the non-fiction text below then answer the questions.**

Birdwatching

Birdwatching, also known as ornithology, is a fun hobby enjoyed by thousands.

Many people like spotting different kinds of birds, in their gardens, in parks and anywhere else outside. Some birds, such as the sparrow, are very common but there are others that are very rare.

Birdwatchers often have binoculars so they can see birds from a distance. They might also have a book to help them identify birds. Sometimes they use a bird hide so birds cannot see them.

It is important to know what birds are visiting different places because this can show how healthy the environment is.

a) Which technical word means 'birdwatching'?

____

b) Which common type of bird is mentioned in the text?

____

c) Why do you think birdwatchers might not want birds to see them?

____

d) Why does the text suggest birdwatching can be important?

____

e) Which two pieces of equipment are mentioned in the text?

____

5 marks

8. Write a sentence that uses a possessive apostrophe for each idea below.

a) a bike belonging to Angus

____

b) a barn belonging to the cow

____

c) a book belonging to Sara

____

3 marks

9. Write a sentence in joined handwriting that uses each word correctly.

brake ____

____

break ____

____

grate ____

____

great ____

____

peace ____

____

piece ____

6 marks

10. Write the definition (the meaning) of each word below.

a) return ____

____

b) antiseptic ____

____

c) autograph ____

____

3 marks

11. Underline the personal pronoun in each sentence.

a) My Aunt Sue said she was once a singer.

b) The boys lost the ball and they were not happy.

c) Zane thinks that he prefers the new carpet.

d) The car will not start because they forgot the petrol.

4 marks

12. Read the list of words with the shun sound at the end. Match each word to its meaning.

extension	finishing something
action	a thing that makes something bigger
completion	doing something, normally to achieve an aim
permission	allowing someone to do something

4 marks

13. Use a dictionary to help you complete the missing word for each definition

a) A tool used for cutting. s ___ i ___ ___ o ___ s

b) The smell of a flower. ___ ___ e n ___

c) A type of sword. ____ ____ i m i ____ ____ r

d) Something very interesting. ____ a s ____ ____ n ____ ____ ing

4 marks

14. Read the text below and then answer the questions.

Jack was always picked first. In every sport, everybody wanted to be on his team. In football he scored lots of goals, in rounders he always hit the ball a long way, and on sports day he was always the fastest runner. Of course, Jack liked this – it made him feel important. He also felt that it gave him great responsibility.

He felt responsible for helping others in his team. If they were not as good as him (most people were not) he would give kind words of encouragement and tell them how well they were trying. You see, Jack did not want others to feel how he felt in Maths and in English when everyone was better than him. He could not understand the numbers or read the words as well as everyone else. Some children poked fun at him. When it came to sport he was determined to show them all. There was more to Jack Richardson than just his skills.

a) Why was Jack always 'picked first'?

____

b) Why did Jack like being good at sport?

____

c) Why did Jack feel that it 'gave him great responsibility'?

____

d) Explain how Jack might have felt in Maths and English.

____

e) What does the last sentence of the text mean?

____

5 marks

15. Read the first two lines of the Haiku below.

October

Leaves falling, cool air,

Golden browns, yellows and reds,

a) Which of the options below would be a suitable final line for the Haiku? Tick the correct option.

Autumn is here again.	In autumn breeze.	As autumn arrives.
☐	☐	☐

b) Explain your choice to part **a)** above.

____ ☐ 2 marks

16. Imagine you are a newsreader. Select the best adverb below to show how each of the news items should be read.

joyfully **sadly** **seriously**

a) Today, there has been a major robbery at the Tower of London. Most of the royal jewels on display have been taken.

____

b) This evening we bring you news of a terrible accident involving several vehicles on the M1 motorway. Early reports show there are many injured.

____

c) We leave you tonight with a rabbit in Scotland who thinks it is a sheep dog. It has been seen chasing sheep and helping the real sheep dogs with their work!

____ ☐ 3 marks

Total: ☐ /65 marks

Maths mixed questions

1. **Here is an addition: 188 + 212 = 400**
   Circle the calculation that can be used to check this addition.

   212 – 188 = **400 + 212 =** **212 + 400 =** **400 – 212 =**

   1 mark

2. **Write the number shown on the abacus in words.**

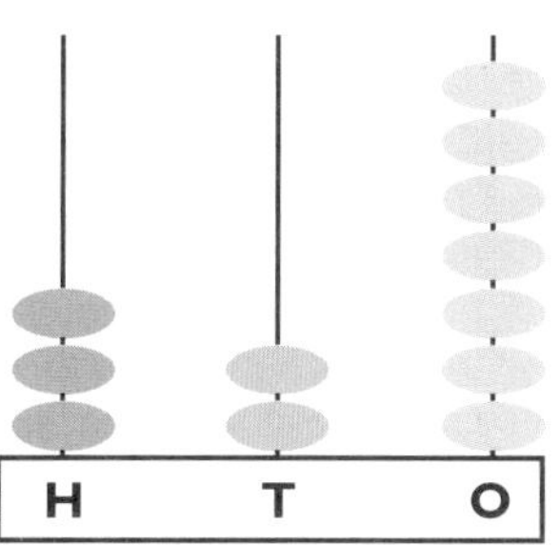

   1 mark

3. **Complete the missing numbers on the number track.**

	14		28		42	49

   3 marks

PS 4. **Mount Everest is 8,848 metres high. Round this height to...**

   a) the nearest 10 metres.

   b) the nearest 100 metres.

   c) the nearest 1,000 metres.

   3 marks

5. **Complete the missing numbers in this multiplication grid.**

×	3	4	5
4	12		20
	18	24	30
8		32	

   4 marks

PS 6. **Maya had £650 in her bank account. She used $\frac{2}{10}$ of her money to buy a new bike.**

   How much money does she have left in her account now? £

   1 mark

7. **Complete the missing numbers.**

   a) ☐ ÷ 10 = 0.7 b) ☐ ÷ 10 = 0.03 c) 78 ÷ ☐ = 0.78

   3 marks

8. Here is a graph showing the growth of a sunflower plant.

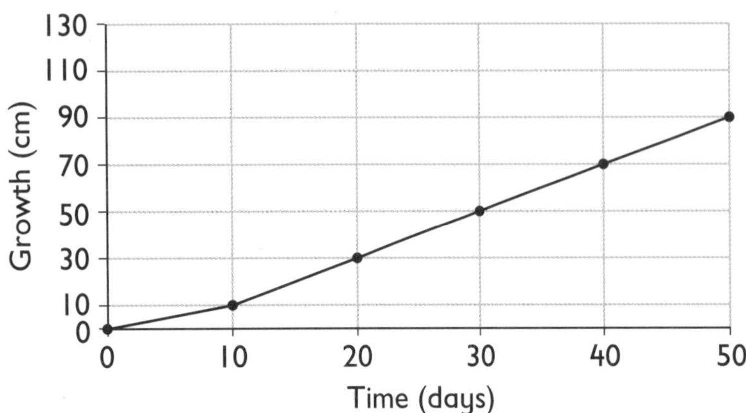

a) What was the growth of the plant at 40 days? ______________

b) How tall did the plant grow between 20 and 50 days? ______________

c) How tall was the plant before it started growing? ______________

3 marks

9. Here are the heights of three towers made from bricks.

Tower	Height
A	1 m 60 cm
B	161 cm
C	1 m 60 mm

Put the towers in order from tallest to shortest.

☐ ☐ ☐

1 mark

10. Complete the calculations.

a)

	Th	H	T	O
	4	2	3	4
+	3	2	4	8

b)

	Th	H	T	O
	7	8	6	4
−	4	2	9	4

2 marks

11. Here is a fraction wall.

Use the fraction wall to help write the missing numbers.

$\frac{8}{\square} = \frac{\square}{5}$

1 mark

PS **12. Class 4H has £75 to spend on books. They buy 5 books that each cost the same price. They have £15 left.**

How much did they spend on each book? £ ☐

I mark

13. Here is a plan of Raj's garden.

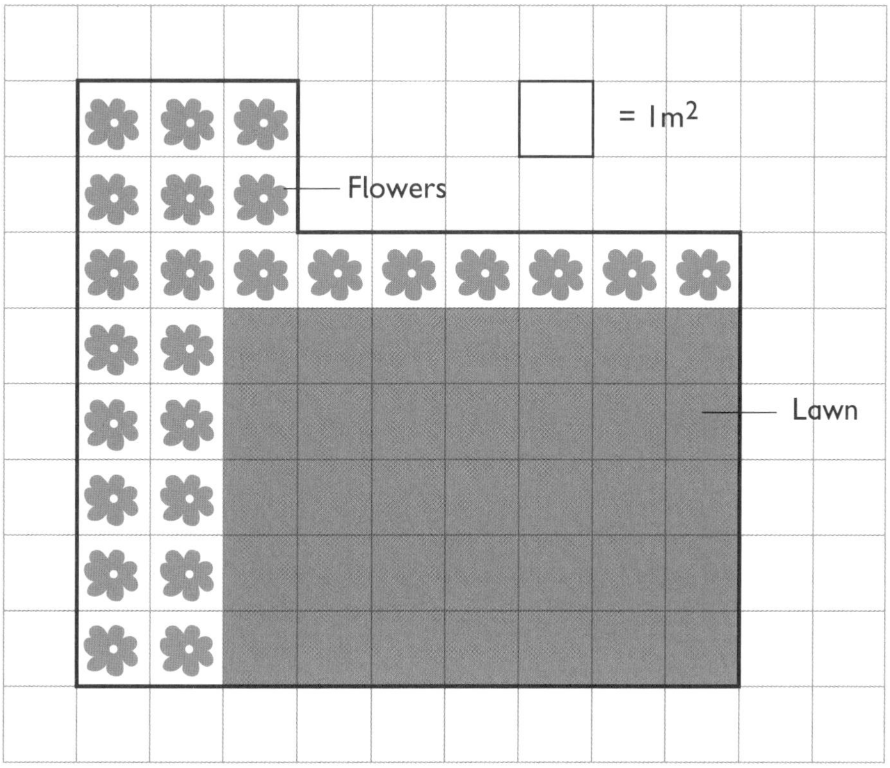

= I m^2

Flowers

Lawn

a) Calculate the area of the lawn. ☐

b) Calculate the perimeter of the whole garden. ☐

c) Find the difference between the area of the flower bed and the lawn. ☐

3 marks

14. List all the factor pairs of 12.

____

I mark

15. Use the symbols <, > or = to complete each statement.

a) $\frac{1}{5}$ of £20 ☐ $\frac{2}{10}$ of £30

b) $\frac{3}{4}$ of £12 ☐ $\frac{1}{3}$ of £27

c) $\frac{5}{8}$ of £32 ☐ $\frac{2}{7}$ of £56

3 marks

PS **16. Gabby compares two different numbers: 13.8 and 13.34**

Gabby says, '13.34 is bigger than 13.8'. Do you agree? Explain your answer.

____

1 mark

17.

Team	Number of house points
Sycamore	■ ■ ■ ■
Beech	■ ■ ▬
Ash	■
Oak	■ ■ ■

Key: ■ = 30 points

a) How many points do Beech and Sycamore teams have altogether? ☐

b) How many more points do the Beech team need to be equal to Oak? ☐

2 marks

PS **18. An ice lolly costs 78p. Find the cost of 3 lollies. Give your answer in pounds and pence.** £ ☐

1 mark

19. $3 - \frac{1}{4} =$ ____________

1 mark

PS **20. Kim has three parcels to post.**

Parcel A weighs 555 g **Parcel B weighs 1.2 kg** **Parcel C weighs 750 g**

a) Order the parcels from lightest to heaviest. ________ ________ ________

b) Find the total weight of all three parcels. ☐

2 marks

21. Complete this calculation.

$$\begin{array}{r} 3\ 8\ 7 \\ \times \quad\ \ 8 \\ \hline \\ \hline \end{array}$$

1 mark

22. Fill in the missing gaps.

There are ☐ seconds in a minute. There are ☐ minutes in an hour.

There are ☐ days in a week. There are ☐ days in a year and ☐ days in a leap year.

5 marks

23. Here is a bar chart and table showing the different ways Year 4 children travel to school.

How Year 4 travel to school

Number of children: 0, 2, 4, 6, 8, 10, 12, 14, 16, 18, 20

Car, Walk, Bus, Bicycle

Transport

Transport	Tally
Car	
Walk	
Bus	
Bicycle	

a) Complete the tally table above using the information from the bar chart.

4 marks

b) What is the most popular way to get to school? ______________

1 mark

c) How many children in total travelled to school?

1 mark

PS **24. One 50p coin is 2 mm thick. Sue has a pile of 50p coins that is 4 cm high.**

How many 50p coins does Sue have in her pile?

1 mark

25. Convert the time on the analogue clock to 24-hour digital time.

Give your answer as a time in the afternoon.

1 mark

26. Round each decimal number to the nearest whole number.

a) 1.9 b) 2.5 c) 2.3

3 marks

27. Here is a coordinate grid.

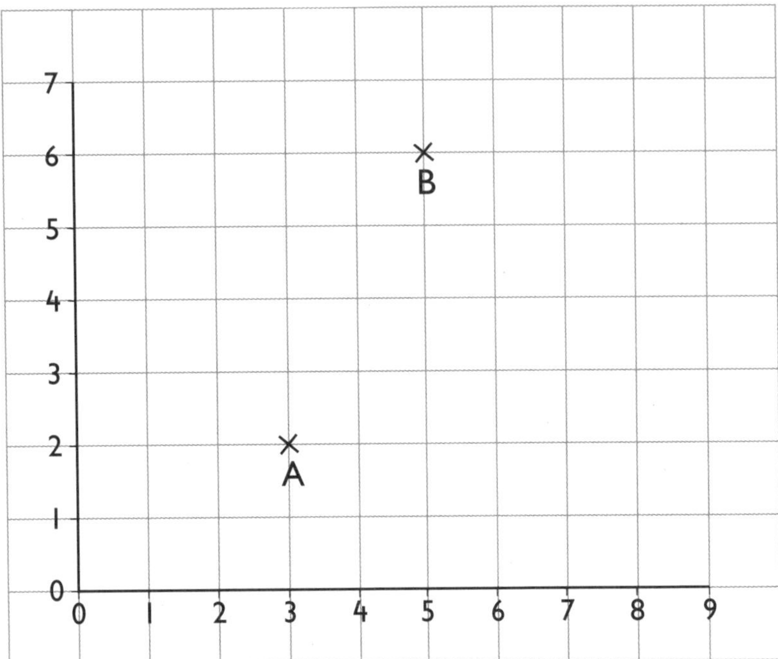

a) Write the coordinates for point A and point B.

2 marks

A: ☐ B: ☐

b) Tamar says that to draw an **isosceles triangle** he needs to plot a third point at (8,2). Do you agree? Explain your answer.

____

1 mark

PS **28. An aeroplane left London with 345 passengers. It stopped off in Paris, where 107 people got off and another 56 people got on board. It then flew to New York.**

How many passengers flew to New York? ☐

1 mark

29. Here is a triangle.

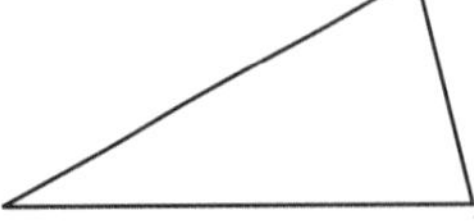

a) Name the type of triangle. ______________________

b) Write two different properties about the triangle, that make it this type of triangle.

____

____

2 marks

PS **30. Jen saved £102. Jen's sister saved twice as much, and Jen's brother saved three times as much as Jen.**

How much have they saved in total? £ ☐

1 mark

31. Tick the statement that is correct:

A An irregular polygon has straight sides and all the lengths are the same size. ☐

B An irregular polygon has mostly straight lines and all the angles are equal. ☐

C An irregular polygon has straight sides and all the angles and lengths are different sizes. ☐

1 mark

PS **32. Priya needs to buy cupcakes for her birthday party.**

Cakes 4 U Bakery
6 cupcakes for £4.20

Calculate the cost to buy exactly 30 cupcakes for her birthday. £ ☐

1 mark

33. Here is a shape on a grid.

Translate the shape 4 squares right and 2 squares up.

1 mark

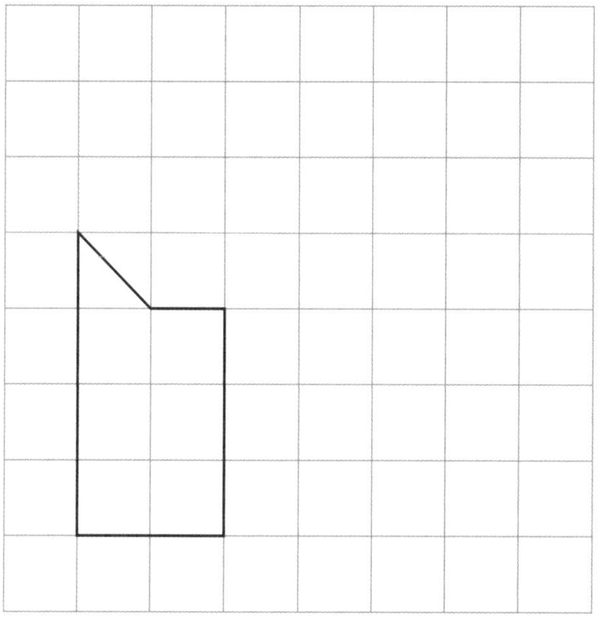

Total: ☐ /65 marks

Answers

ENGLISH

Page 5

Challenge 1

1. **a)** super **b)** anti
   c) sub **d)** re

Challenge 2

1. **a)** subway
   b) refresh
   c) imperfect
   d) submarine
   e) antifreeze

Challenge 3

1. **Accept answers which show understanding that the prefix changed the meaning of the root word. Examples:**
   a) put or go under water
   b) not patient
   c) not sociable

Page 7

Challenge 1

1. **a)** relaxation – rest
   b) temptation – something hard to resist
   c) formation – things in order
   d) presentation – something to show

Challenge 2

1. **a)** invention – something new
   b) exception – something that does not follow a rule
   c) politician – someone who speaks out about important issues
   d) musician – somebody who plays an instrument

Challenge 3

1. **a)** preparation
   b) admiration
   c) expectation
   d) imagination

Page 9

Challenge 1

1. **a)** dialogue
   b) opaque
   c) antique
   d) vague

Challenge 2

1. **a)** parachute
   b) architect
   c) character
   d) machine

Challenge 3

1. **Accept any reasonably accurate definition. Examples:**
   a) somebody who uses science
   b) to go up
   c) a slim 'moon' shape
   d) beautiful natural scenery

Page 11

Challenge 1

1. **a)** Fairytale
   b) Adventure Story
   c) Science Fiction

Challenge 2

1. **a)** Historical fiction
   b) It is set in the past – cobbled streets, sweeping chimneys (Alf is a boy chimney sweep).

Challenge 3

1. Alf – boy, chimney sweep, skinny, poor;
   Mr Gresty – looks mean, doesn't care about Alf

Page 13

Challenge 1

1. **a)** Line 1: 5, Line 2: 7, Line 3: 5
   b) **Accept either**: Traffic; Fear of being late

Challenge 2

1. **a)** looking at the sky
   b) to help show that they are lying on the ground
   c) stars

Challenge 3

1. Line 2: not stopping, going on and on
   Line 4: the train is going so fast that everything looks like a blur.

Page 15

Challenge 1

1. bad, destroying

Challenge 2

1. **a)** upset and/or scared
   b) he is naughty

Challenge 3

1. **Accept any suitable answers. Examples:**
   a) A large smile spread across Cam's face.
   b) Tears rolled down Anil's cheeks.

Page 17
Challenge 1
1. **a)** angrily
   b) sadly
   c) quietly

Challenge 2
1. **Accept any reasonable answer. Examples:**
   a) excitedly
   b) angrily
   c) sadly

Challenge 3
1. **The answer should make reference to the speed of the ball and then the fact that it had stopped, e.g. fast and excited at first then slow and quiet when it has stopped.**

Page 19
Challenge 1
1. **a)** third person writing **('it' is referring to the water vapour)**
   b) technical words
   c) formal language **('forming clouds' is a more formal way of saying 'making clouds')**

Challenge 2
1. **a)** made of
   b) areas of water, e.g. oceans, lakes, rivers

Challenge 3
1. **a)** it warms up/heat from the sun
   b) it cools down (as it rises)

Page 21
Challenge 1
1. **Accept an answer that lists the key points (not detail) telling what happens in the correct order.**

Challenge 2
1. The road will pass through Old Nook; Old Nook is home to rare bats. **(All other information is assumed, not fact.)**

Challenge 3
1. **a)** Wildlife in Old Nook will be damaged.
   b) **Accept any one from:** It will cut traffic at Greenway; It will bring jobs: It will reduce journey time.

Pages 22–25
Progress test 1: English
1. **a)** anti
   b) super
   c) inter
   d) re
   e) sub
2. **a)** admiration
   b) invitation
   c) information
   d) preparation
   e) transportation
3. **a)** intrigue
   b) meringue
   c) vague
   d) fatigue
   e) colleague
4. **Accept any correct definitions. Examples:**
   a) used to stop a ship/boat moving
   b) someone who designs buildings/structures
   c) facial hair beneath the nose
   d) a booklet usually selling things
   e) something designed to do or make something
   f) a recurring part of a song or poem
5. **a)** science fiction
   b) it is set in space/another world
   c) she is determined/tries hard (never gives up)
6. **a)** the movement is very slow
   b) slugs
   c) Its structure: line 1 has 5 syllables, line 2 has 7 syllables and line 3 has 5 syllables.
7. **Accept any suitable answer. Examples:**
   a) Jess' stomach rumbled.
   b) Eli jumped up and down, unable to keep still.
8. **Accept any suitable answer. Examples:**
   a) politely
   b) moaning
   c) angrily
9. **a)** **Accept any two from:** brilliant Blackpool; beaches are big and spacious; has a motorway nearby making it really easy to get to.
   b) ii) ✓

MATHS
Page 27
Challenge 1
1. **a)** 300 **b)** 500 **c)** 900 **d)** 700
2. **a)** 2,000 **b)** 4,000 **c)** 6,000 **d)** 8,000
3. **a)** V **b)** L **c)** XXXV **d)** XIX

Challenge 2

1.

Abacus	Th H T O	Th H T O	Th H T O
Number in numerals	**1,446**	6,505	**9,390**
Number in words	**One thousand, four hundred and forty-six**	**Six thousand, five hundred and five**	Nine thousand, three hundred and ninety

Challenge 3

1. **a)** 65
   b) 9
   c) 100
2. Both✓. The numbers are the same because sixteen ones is the same as one ten and six ones.

Page 29

Challenge 1

1. **a)** 4,870, 4,910, 5,555, 5,708
   b) 6,061, 6,179, 6,862, 6,990
2. **a)** 50
   b) 70
   c) 90
3. **a)** 100
   b) 500
   c) 300
4. **a)** 1,000
   b) 4,000
   c) 3,000

Challenge 2

1. **a)** **Accept:** 5,**2**16, 5,**1**16 or 5,**0**16
   b) **Accept:** **1**,586, **2**,586, **3**,586, **4**,586 or **5**,586

2.

Number	Rounded to the nearest 10	Rounded to the nearest 100	Rounded to the nearest 1,000
4,567	**4,570**	4,600	**5,000**
3,291	3,290	**3,300**	**3,000**

Challenge 3

1. **a)** 9,431
   b) 1,349
   c) 1,943 or 1,934

Page 31
Challenge 1

1. **a)** 7,766
   b) 10,070
   c) 2,250
   d) 3,950
2. **a)** 2,565
   b) 6,650
   c) 4,642
   d) 8,121

Challenge 2

1.

1,000 more	Start number	1,000 less
8,894	7,894	**6,894**
4,539	**3,539**	**2,539**
2,345	**1,345**	345

2. **a)** −5°C
   b) 1°C

Challenge 3

1. B✓ C✓ **(both correct for 1 mark)**
2. No. 7 degrees less than 5 degrees is −2 degrees.

Page 33
Challenge 1

1. **a)** 0, 1,000, **2,000**, 3,000, 4,000, **5,000**
   b) 0, 25, **50**, 75, 100, **125**
   c) 0, 6, 12, 18, **24, 30**
   d) 0, 9, **18,** 27, **36,** 45

Challenge 2

1. **a)** 160
   b) 16
   c) 32
2. **a)** 6
   b) 1,000
   c) 7
   d) 25

Challenge 3

1. **a)** False ✓ because they can also end in 0
   b) True ✓ because they all end in 0
   c) False ✓ because 14, 28, 42, 56, 70, 84 are multiples of 7 and they are all even numbers
   d) False ✓ because 9 × 12 = 108

Page 35
Challenge 1

1. **a)** 1,100
   b) 1,460
   c) 1,310
   d) 4,200
   e) 7,800
   f) 7,090
   g) 13,705
   h) 2,610

Challenge 2

1. **a)** Estimate: 5,050; Answer: 4,805; Check: 4,805 − 48 = 4,757
   b) Estimate: 5,300; Answer: 5,563; Check: 5,563 − 286 = 5,277
   c) Estimate: 9,000; Answer: 9,690; Check: 9,690 − 3,428 = 6,262
   d) Estimate: 4,000; Answer: 4,052; Check: 4,052 − 1,775 = 2,277

Challenge 3

1. **a)** 9,040 fans
   b) 8,340 science books
2.

	13,131		
	6,075	7,056	
2,627	3,448	**3,608**	
1,524	1,103	2,345	1,263

Page 37
Challenge 1

1. **a)** 1,100
   b) 3,080
   c) 2,280
   d) 1,900
   e) 6,940
   f) 4,820
   g) 5,390
   h) 5,800

Challenge 2

1. a) Estimate: 1,800; Answer: 1,452; Check: 1,452 + 243 = 1,695
   b) Estimate: 6,000; Answer: 6,387; Check: 6,387 + 819 = 7,206
   c) Estimate: 2,000; Answer: 1,816; Check: 1,816 + 5,254 = 7,070
   d) Estimate: 1,000; Answer: 1,146; Check: 1,146 + 1,022 = 2,168

Challenge 3

1. a) 3,908 gold coins
   b) 732 sheets of paper

Page 39

Challenge 1

1. a)

×	4
4	**16**
7	**28**
9	**36**
12	**48**

b)

×	6
3	**18**
6	**36**
8	**48**
9	**54**

c)

×	8
5	**40**
9	**72**
6	**48**
7	**56**

d)

×	5
5	**25**
6	**30**
12	**60**
7	**35**

e)

×	7
7	**49**
9	**63**
4	**28**
3	**21**

2. a) 3 × 5 circled
   b) 7 × 3 circled

Challenge 2

1. a) 7
   b) 12
   c) 6
   d) 8
   e) 8
   f) 12
2. a) 42 b) 120 c) 216

Challenge 3

1. a) 60, 300, 30
   b) 70, 2,800
2. No. There are more than 2 factor pairs. There are also 5 × 6 and 10 × 3.

Page 41

Challenge 1

1. a) 204
   b) 296
   c) 348
   d) 2,268
   e) 432
   f) 1,868
2. a) 13
   b) 17
   c) 13
   d) 287
   e) 198
   f) 114

Challenge 2

1. a) 243 b) 433

Challenge 3

1. a) False
   b) False
   c) No. Arun is wrong because 321 ÷ 3 equals 107 whilst 152 × 3 equals 456, so they are not the same.

Page 43

Challenge 1

1. 1,380 cm
2. 28
3. 1,435 kg

Challenge 2

1. 8 combinations

Trainers	Socks
grey	red
grey	blue
grey	black
grey	green
white	red
white	blue
white	black
white	green

Challenge 3

1. 8 × 36 = 288; 288 × 9 = 2,592
2. 6 × 64 = 384; 4 × 78 = 312; 312 + 384 = 696

Pages 44–47
Progress test 2: Maths

1. 1,412 > 290 > 250 > 204
2. 2,017 points
3. One thousand, one hundred and twenty-two
4.

×	3	4	5
4	12	**16**	20
6	18	24	30
8	**24**	32	**40**

5. **a)** 6°C
   b) 11°C
6. 100
7. 428 stickers
8. **a)** <
   b) >
   c) <
9. **a)** 6,000 km
   b) 7,000 km
   c) 5,000 km
10. **a)** 5,660
    b) 3,265
11. 1,127
12. circled: 20 × 3, 6 × 10 × 1
13. L
14. 14
15. 1,320; 3,540; 5,567; 6,568; 7,981; 7,993
16. 1 × 48; 2 × 24; 3 × 16; 4 × 12; 6 × 8 (**All correct for 1 mark**)
17. No. 75 is a multiple of 25 and is an odd number.
18. 6,654 + 6,540 = 13,194; 13,194 – 6,855 = 6,339 metres
19. chicken + apple
    chicken + ice cream
    tofu + apple
    tofu + ice cream
20.

	5	7	9	1
	2	4	2	**1**
+	3	**8**	7	7
1	2	0	8	9

ENGLISH

Page 49
Challenge 1

1. **All letters to be correctly formed and joined, with consistent length and direction of ascenders and descenders.**

Challenge 2

1. **All letters to be correctly formed and joined, with consistent length and direction of ascenders and descenders. Accept correct definition for each word. Examples:**
   scene – a place where something happens; part of a play or film
   seen – the past tense of the verb 'see'
   meat – flesh of an animal
   meet – when people get together
   rein – a strap for holding onto a horse
   rain – water falling from the sky

Challenge 3

1. **All letters to be correctly formed and joined, with consistent length and direction of ascenders and descenders. Accept suitable sentences. Examples:**
   missed – We missed the bus because we were late.
   mist – There was a fine mist over the lake.

Page 51
Challenge 1

1. immortal, illegal, incorrect, international, irregular

Challenge 2

1. **a)** irresponsible
   b) impatient
   c) inactive
   d) illegal
   e) imperfect

Challenge 3

1. inregular should be irregular; ilpossible should be impossible; imcorrect should be incorrect
2. **a)** illogical **b)** inaccurate

Page 53
Challenge 1

1. **a)** measure
   b) structure
   c) departure
   d) leisure

Challenge 2

1. **a)** adventure
   b) creature
   c) pleasure
   d) mixture

Challenge 3

1. **Each sentence to use the given word in an appropriate way. Examples:**
   a) The bridge was a fantastic structure.
   b) A main feature of the garden was the fountain.
   c) Measure out the ingredients carefully.
   d) The flight was nearly ready for departure.
   e) The team had just one remaining fixture to play.

Page 55
Challenge 1

1. zhun ending – erosion, vision, evasion, illusion
   shun ending – admission, tension, mansion, musician

Challenge 2

1. **a)** invasion
   b) conclusion
   c) confusion
   d) collision
   e) exclusion
   f) delusion

Challenge 3

1. **Each sentence should use the given word in an appropriate and accurate way. Examples:**
   a) The cliffs were collapsing because of erosion.
   b) They finally made a decision about their holiday.
   c) There was a collision when the car skidded on the ice.
   d) There was some confusion about the theatre tickets.

Page 57
Challenge 1

1. **Each sentence should contain at least one adjective and fit appropriately with the existing sentences.**

Challenge 2

1. **Each sentence should contain at least one adjective and fit appropriately with the existing sentences.**

Challenge 3

1. **Notes should suggest what might happen as the problem is solved and the story ends.**

Page 59
Challenge 1

1. Paragraph 1: The puppy was…
   Paragraph 2: Lois had wanted …
   Paragraph 3: Mum had made …

Challenge 2

1. **First paragraph is about her lessons. Second paragraph is about her friends. Additional two sentences should fit appropriately with each paragraph.**

Challenge 3

1. **Accept any reasonable justification of the split as above. Example:**
   Each paragraph is about a different part of Eva's school life. The information about lessons is organised into one paragraph and the information about her friends is organised into another.

Page 61
Challenge 1

1. Paragraph 1 – different types of tropical fish
   Paragraph 2 – choosing a fish tank
   Paragraph 3 – water temperature

Challenge 2

1. **Accept an appropriate subheading for each, which fits with the paragraphs. Examples:**
   a) My class
   b) Lessons

Challenge 3

1. **Accept appropriate content for each subheading. Examples:**
   a) 1 – who I live with, 2 – other family
   b) 1 and 2 – any two hobbies
   c) 1 and 2 – any two ambitions

Page 63
Challenge 1

1. **Accept appropriate words that fit in with the text and are more interesting. Examples:** nice – beautiful, well – magnificently, bright – burning, carefully – tightly, big – vast

Challenge 2

1. The horse did not slow as the sun moved closer to the horizon⊙Shadows grew longer and dusk becameⓚnight. Onwards they sped, towards the dark shape of mountins in the distance. There amazing beast kept going although it was getting tired.ⓔach child starⓡed at the stars. They saw familiar shapes in the heavens and knew they were nearly their.

Challenge 3

1. First sentence: As the sun moved closer to the horizon, the horse did not slow.
   Fourth sentence: Although it was getting tired, their amazing beast kept going.

Pages 64–67
Progress test 3: English

1. **a)** Answer should refer to patiently waiting for the ice-cream to be ready.
   b) Time passes slowly when waiting for the ice-cream.
   c) To make the reader wait patiently to find out what the poem is about.
2. **a)** to go down
   b) very interesting
   c) a view or place
   d) to go up
3. **All letters to be correctly formed and joined, with consistent length and direction of ascenders and descenders.**
4. **a)** illegible
   b) impossible
   c) immature
   d) irrelevant
   e) irregular
5. **Each sentence should use the given word in an appropriate and accurate way. Examples:**
   a) There was an invasion of ants in the school kitchen.
   b) The decision was made to close the kitchen.
   c) There was confusion about the new lunch arrangements.
   d) There was an explosion at the firework factory.
   e) There was a collision between a bus and a lorry.
6. **a)** treasure
   b) departure
   c) nature
   d) enclosure
   e) measure
   f) picture
7. **a) Notes should show an idea of how the story is resolved and how the story ends. Examples:**
   Resolution: the Prince searches for the owner of the slipper and finds Cinderella.
   Ending: They get married/live happily ever after.
   b) Answer should include at least one sentence and adjective describing what the slipper looked like, and at least one sentence and adjective describing how it felt. Examples:
   It looked beautiful as the light made it sparkle and shine. It felt so light and precious in his hands.
8. **First paragraph is about when/how they started flying kites. Second paragraph is about Kite Club. Additional two sentences should fit appropriately with each paragraph.**
9. **Accept appropriate words that fit with the text and are more interesting. Examples:**
   shiny – gleaming, big – loud, fast – speedy, lovely – fantastic, good – brilliant, looked – gazed

MATHS
Page 69
Challenge 1

1. **a)** $\frac{1}{3} = \frac{2}{6} = \frac{4}{12}$
   b) $\frac{1}{2} = \frac{2}{4} = \frac{4}{8}$
   c) $\frac{3}{5} = \frac{6}{10}$
   d) $\frac{9}{12} = \frac{3}{4} = \frac{6}{8}$
2. **a)** Accept: $\frac{5}{10}$ or $\frac{1}{2}$
   b) Accept: $\frac{9}{6}$ or $1\frac{3}{6}$ or $1\frac{1}{2}$
   c) Accept: $\frac{6}{12}$ or $\frac{1}{2}$
   d) $\frac{7}{8}$
   e) Accept: $\frac{9}{5}$ or $1\frac{4}{5}$
   f) $\frac{3}{7}$

Challenge 2

1. **a)** 68
   b) 136
   c) 170

2. £375
3. a) $\frac{2}{9}$
   b) $\frac{3}{9}$
   c) $\frac{19}{9} = 2\frac{1}{9}$

Challenge 3
1. a) 150
   b) 64
   c) 400
2. £5

Page 71
Challenge 1
1. $\frac{26}{100}, \frac{30}{100}, \frac{33}{100}$
2. a) 0.6
   b) 0.09
   c) 6.4
   d) 0.78

Challenge 2
1. circled: 3 ÷ 100, 0.3 ÷ 10 (**both circled for 1 mark**)
2. a) 10
   b) 100
   c) 100
   d) 10

Challenge 3
1. a) 0.75 cm
   b) 74.25 cm

Page 73
Challenge 1
1. a) 0.5
   b) 0.1
   c) 0.75
   d) 0.25
   e) 0.01
2. 6.8 to 7; 3.5 to 4; 1.5 to 2; 1.2 to 1; 4.9 to 5; 5.7 to 6; 3.2 to 3

Challenge 2
1. a) >
   b) <
   c) <
   d) <
   e) >
   f) <
2. No. Chestnut raised the most because £44.60 is more than £43.88. Oak raised the least.

Challenge 3
1. 4 m
2. £3.01

Page 75
Challenge 1
1. a) 110 g
   b) 350 ml
   c) 200 cm
2. a) 4,000 g
   b) 6,200 ml
   c) 1,800 m
   d) 0.5 kg
   e) 3,700 g
   f) 420 cm

Challenge 2
1. a) =
   b) >
   c) =
2. a) 900 g
   b) 1,100 g
   c) 250 g

Challenge 3
1. a) 1.5 kg
   b) 1.5 m and 3 m
   c) Yes. It will fit because 520 mm + 520 mm = 1,040 mm = 104 cm. 104 cm is the same as 1.04 m which is less than 1.1 m.

Page 77
Challenge 1
1. 24 cm
2. 13 cm^2

Challenge 2
1. a) 21 m^2
   b) Multiply the length by the width, which is 7 × 3 = 21
   c) 28 m

Challenge 3
1. 4 cm

Page 79
Challenge 1
1. a) £1.38
   b) £2.52
2. a) £4.03; £4.35; £4.40; £4.53
   b) £2.90; £2.99; £9.02; £9.20

Challenge 2
1. a) £5.41
   b) £12.35
   c) £2.75 + £3.86 + £1.55 = £8.16;
      £10 − £8.16 = £1.84

Challenge 3
1. 5 car models
2. £15.25 + £30.50 + £61 = £106.75

Page 81
Challenge 1
1. a) 48 hours
   b) 180 minutes
   c) 6 months
   d) 4 years
2. a) Quarter to four
   b) Twenty-five minutes past twelve
   c) Eighteen minutes to six

Challenge 2
1. a) 04:09
   b) 20:02
2. 100 minutes or 1 hour 40 minutes

Challenge 3
1. 5 hours and 20 minutes
2. No. The next tournament will be in 2024 because there is a leap year every four years.

Page 83
Challenge 1
1. a) C and D
   b) A and G
2. F

Challenge 2
1.

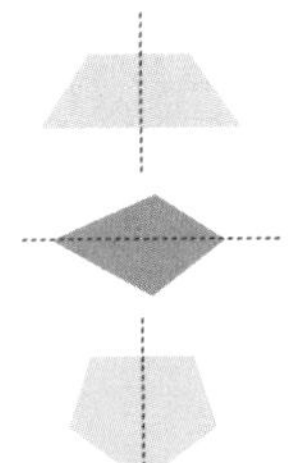

2.

	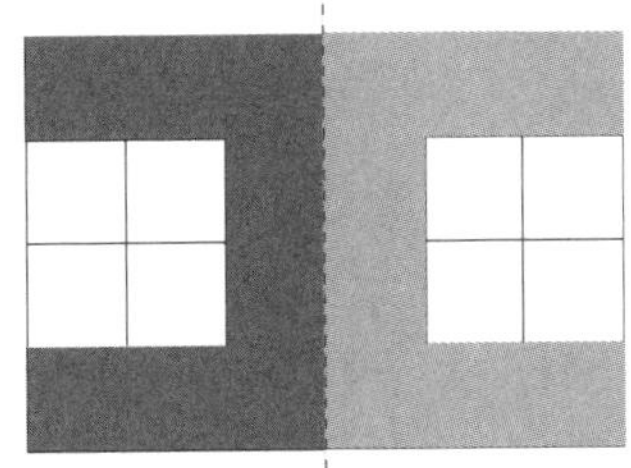	
Name	Rhombus	Triangle
Is it a quadrilateral?	Yes	No
Number of pairs of parallel lines	2	0

Challenge 3
1. a)

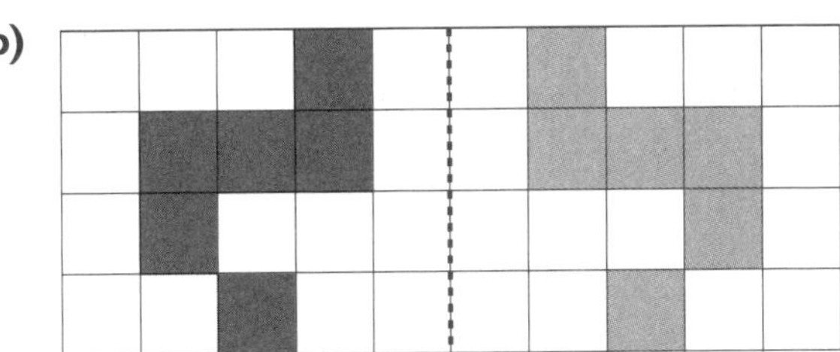

b)

Page 85
Challenge 1
1. a) C
   b) B
   c) A
2. C, B, D, A, E

Challenge 2
1–3. Examples

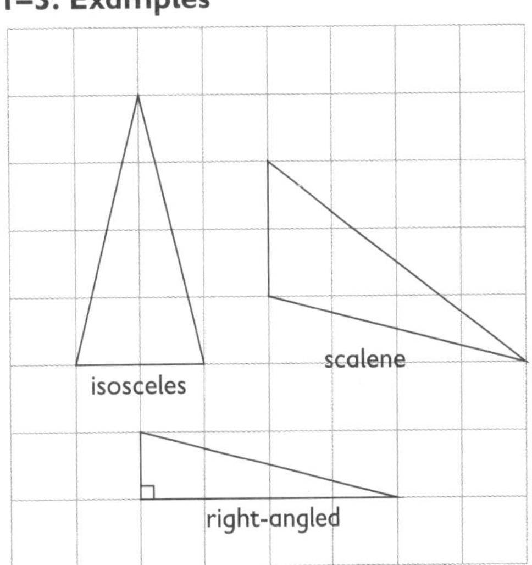

Challenge 3

1. No. It is an obtuse angle because the hour hand has gone past 3 o'clock but is before 6 o'clock.

Page 87

Challenge 1

1. a) (4,2)
   b) (7,4)
   c) (2,5)
   d) (5,4)
   e) (0,3)
   f) (9,0)

Challenge 2

1. a) 2 right, 2 down
   b) 4 left, 1 up
   c) 2 right, 2 up
   d) 6 left, 3 up

Challenge 3

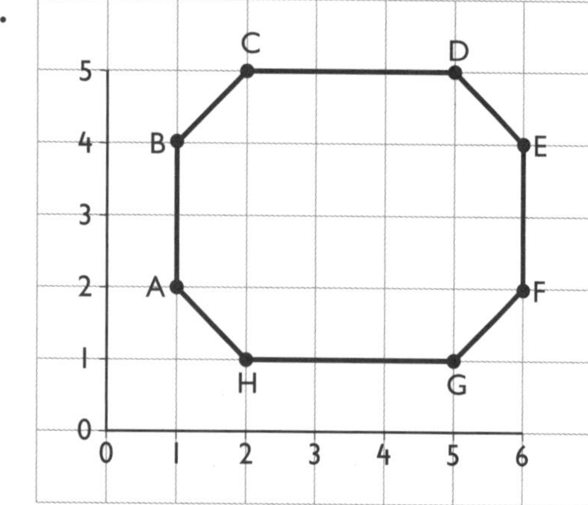

2. Octagon

Page 89

Challenge 1

1. a) Pasta
   b) Katie
   c) Kamal

Challenge 2

1. a) 60
   b) No. They sold 42 pizzas because if $\frac{1}{2}$ symbol = 6 pizzas then one whole symbol = 12 pizzas. 12 × 3 = 36; 36 + 6 = 42
   c) *Fast Pizza* = 54, *Cheesy Pizza* = 33; 54 − 33 = 21 more pizzas

Challenge 3

1. a) 200 letters
   b)

Page 91

Challenge 1

1. a) Max
   b) 10

Challenge 2

1. a) Day 8
   b) 8 cm
   c) 8 cm

Challenge 3

1. 9 to 10 a.m, 11 a.m. to 12 noon, 1 to 2 p.m.

Pages 92–95

Progress test 4: Maths

1. a) $\frac{13}{100}$; $\frac{14}{100}$
   b) 0.5, 0.6
2. $7\,m^2$
3. 9p
4. 507
5. a) 40
   b) 190
   c) 300
6. £1,467
7. a) 5,800
   b) 3,574
8. 4,903; 4,681; 4,590; 4,508; 4,399; 4,182
9. a) $\frac{1}{5} = \frac{2}{10} = \frac{4}{20}$
   b) $\frac{1}{2} = \frac{3}{6} = \frac{4}{8}$
10. 9 × 4 × 8 ✓
11. a) £5.15
    b) £4.80
12. $\frac{1}{2}$ to 0.5; $\frac{1}{5}$ to 0.2; $\frac{3}{4}$ to 0.75; $\frac{1}{100}$ to 0.01
13. 12 stickers
14. a) $\frac{11}{10}$ or $1\frac{1}{10}$
    b) $\frac{8}{12}$
    c) $\frac{25}{100}$
15. Three thousand, two hundred and eleven

16.

	Regular	Not regular
Quadrilateral	F	B
Not a quadrilateral	A, C	D, E

17. $\frac{3}{12}$

18. 60 g berries; 50 ml milk; 25 g of yoghurt; 3.5 g of sugar

19. a) B; D; A; C

b) Angle A is a right angle; Angle B is an acute angle; Angle C is an obtuse angle.

20.

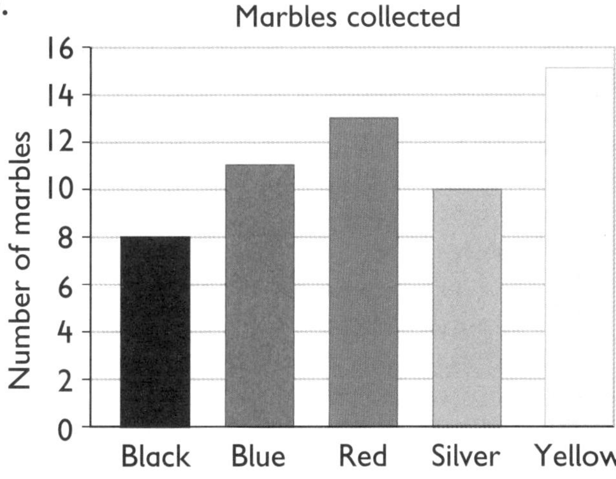

ENGLISH

Page 97

Challenge 1

1. a) They had (a) great time <u>when</u> they went to (the) circus.

b) School will open <u>if</u> we can clear (this) snow.

c) Everyone jumped <u>when</u> Bruce dropped (his) pan.

d) We washed (our) hands <u>and</u> then went for (our) lunch.

e) We had (a) new teacher today <u>because</u> Mr White was ill.

Challenge 2

1. a) the team wins today.

b) I am full.

c) the journey is over.

d) I prefer honey.

Challenge 3

1. a) when (or because)

b) if (or when)

c) because/as

d) when (or after)

2. Example sentences:

a) I like PE **but** I prefer art.

b) **Although** it is a mile away, I always walk to school.

c) We can eat lunch outside **when** it is a sunny day.

d) I take my hockey stick **if** there is hockey practice.

Page 99

Challenge 1

1. a) <u>After the game</u>, the team lifted the trophy.

b) <u>Under the bed</u>, she found an old newspaper.

c) <u>Later</u>, there will be free sweets at the disco.

d) <u>Originally</u>, they had planned to walk to school.

Challenge 2

1. a) I saw some creepy creatures.

b) we watched a great film.

c) he saw a jellyfish.

Challenge 3

1. a) After lunch, we went to the shops.

b) When we were on the ferry, we saw whales.

c) On the way home, I got some fish and chips.

d) Straight after our football match, it rained.

e) Before you go outside, you need your coat on.

Page 101

Challenge 1

1. school field, bathroom door, log fire, train station, tennis court

Challenge 2

1. a) There was <u>a hat on the empty chair</u>.

b) It was <u>a red, felt hat</u>.

c) My cousin has <u>an amazing guitar</u>.

d) We like <u>the food in the new café in town</u>.

Challenge 3

1. Accept appropriate endings (that include a prepositional phrase) for each sentence. Examples:

a) over the fence.

b) in the countryside.

c) on the crowd.

d) under the bridge.

2. Example answers:

a) gold **b)** shopping **c)** football **d)** kitchen

Page 103

Challenge 1

1. **a)** "This is a lovely picture," said Mr Harb.
   b) "Let's get going," urged Dad.
   c) "What time is the last train?" asked the lady.

Challenge 2

1. **a)** "The taxi is here," said Ella.
   b) Sophie said, "Look at how busy the beach is."
   c) "What would you like to drink?" asked the waiter.
   d) Connie asked, "Who would like to play with me?"

Challenge 3

1. **Accept a suitable direct speech sentence. Examples:**
   a) "You cannot play," said Abbie to her brother.
   b) "Can you help with my homework?" Carlo asked his sister.
   c) "I will see you soon," said Joe to his cousin.

Page 105

Challenge 1

1. **a)** Suzy ate the bread because she was hungry.
   b) Daisy had to walk to school when she moved house.
   c) Luke and Amy were lost and they began to cry.
   d) The creature stared and it looked fierce.

Challenge 2

1. **a)** hers
   b) ours
   c) yours
   d) his

Challenge 3

1. Stan went to **his** den. **He** stayed in **it** for hours. It was lunchtime when **he** appeared. Stan asked **his mum** what was for lunch. **She** asked **him** what **he** would like for **his** lunch.

Page 107

Challenge 1

1. **a)** ship's
   b) Frank's
   c) man's
   d) James'

Challenge 2

1. **a)** Evie's
   b) dog's
   c) its
   d) girls'

Challenge 3

1. **Each sentence must make sense and include the correct possessive apostrophe. Examples:**
   a) girl's cat
   b) bus' wheel
   c) Ross' toy
   d) Mia's book
   c) boys' football

Pages 108–111

Progress test 5: English

1. **a)** They borded the boat as the sun started to set and heded out to see. All was calm and they soon lowerd the fishing nets. Before midnight they had plenty of fish and decided to head home. By now the sea was getting rough as a strong wind blew into them. rain started and they culd no longer see the lights from the shore. The boat was tosed up and down for several hours.
   b) First sentence: As the sun started to set, they boarded the boat and headed out to sea.
   Last sentence: For several hours, the boat was tossed up and down.
2. **Accept any suitable headings. Examples:**
   a) Choosing a dog
   b) Looking after a dog
3. **a)** preparation – something that is ready or being got ready
   b) adoration – loving something
   c) imagination – thinking about new or creative things
4. **a)** you have got changed.
   b) they look a little hard.
   c) you eat your soup.
   d) it is healthy.
5. **a)** After the rain, there was a rainbow.
   b) When he saw the clown, Jack jumped.
   c) When I fell over, I hurt my leg.
   d) Before it got so windy, it was a lovely day.
6. **Accept suitable prepositional phases. Examples:**
   a) in the box / on her feet.
   b) on the ocean / on the sea.
   c) on the rooftops / on the garden.
7. **a)** his
   b) yours
   c) theirs
   d) hers

8. **a)** bees'
b) Ella's
c) ladies'
d) hotel's
9. Mum went to **her** work because **she** had left her phone behind. **Her** phone was where **she** had left **it** on **her** desk. Mum's desk was very tidy. **It** looked like **it** been cleaned by the cleaners. **They** were very kind.
10. church bells, garden shed, water jug, star prize, fish tank
11. **a)** The clouds are big/large (or tall).
b) The sea is getting rough.
c) Angry (and crashing)
d) It is a thunderstorm (there is thunder and lightning).
12. **a)** unique **b)** colleague **c)** fatigue **d)** technique

English mixed questions
Pages 112–118

1. **a)** **Accept either:** we saw a police car; we had a quick snack.
b) we wrap up warm.
c) some people were fishing.
d) everyone was full.
e) **Accept either:** we had a quick snack; we saw a police car.
2. **a)** A fish lived under the deep blue sea.
b) It was a green, spotty fish.
c) The fish hid under large rocks.
d) It likes to be away from the nipping crabs.
e) There was a large, vicious crab.
3. **a)** "Work on your own," said the teacher.
b) "Do you want help with lunch, Mum?" asked James.
c) "I am going on holiday," said Elsa.
d) "When will we get home?" asked Simone.
4. **a)** Sam's
b) Bess'
c) its
d) Mack's
5. **a)** yours
b) his
c) theirs
d) ours
6. **a)** As we got there, the boat arrived.
b) When we had our fifth birthdays, there were lots of parties.
c) When he heard his team had won, Dan did a crazy dance.
d) When it was really cold, only two people went outside.
7. **a)** ornithology
b) sparrow
c) so they don't get scared
d) it can show how healthy the environment is
e) book, binoculars **(both answers correct for 1 mark)**
8. **Each sentence must include:**
a) Angus' bike
b) the cow's barn
c) Sara's book
9. **All letters must be formed correctly and joined. Sentences must use the given word correctly. Examples:**
brake – Sam forgot to use his brake and crashed his bike.
break – The window will break if the ball keeps hitting it.
grate – The fire was burning brightly in the grate.
great – There are great plans for the leisure centre.
peace – She enjoyed the peace by the lakeside.
piece – A piece of glass lay on the floor.
10. **a)** to go back
b) against septic – used to prevent something becoming septic
c) a person's signature
11. **a)** My Aunt Sue said she was once a singer.
b) The boys lost the ball and they were not happy.
c) Zane thinks that he prefers the new carpet.
d) The car will not start because they forgot the petrol.
12. extension – a thing that makes something bigger
action – doing something, normally to achieve an aim
completion – finishing something
permission – allowing someone to do something
13. **a)** scissors **b)** scent **c)** scimitar **d)** fascinating
14. **a)** He was good at sports.
b) It made him feel important.
c) Because he was good he wanted to help others.
d) He might have felt that he was not very clever.
e) He did not just have sports skills, he was also very kind.
15. **a)** As Autumn arrives.✓
b) It is the only choice with the five syllables, which are required for the last line of the poem.
16. **a)** seriously **b)** sadly **c)** joyfully

Pages 119–125
Maths mixed questions

1. circled: 400 – 212 =
2. Three hundred and twenty-seven
3. 7, 21, 35
4. **a)** 8,850 m
b) 8,800 m
c) 9,000 m

5.

×	3	4	5
4	12	**16**	20
6	18	24	30
8	**24**	32	**40**

6. £520
7. **a)** 7
b) 0.3
c) 100
8. **a)** 70 cm
b) 60 cm
c) 0 cm
9. B, A, C
10. **a)** 7,482
b) 3,570
11. $\frac{8}{10} = \frac{4}{5}$
12. £12
13. **a)** 35 m^2
b) 34 m
c) 10 m^2
14. 12 × 1, 6 × 2, 3 × 4
15. **a)** $<$
b) $=$
c) $>$
16. No. 13.8 is bigger than 13.34 as it has a greater value tenth digit.
17. **a)** 195
b) 15
18. £2.34
19. $2\frac{3}{4}$
20. **a)** A, C, B
b) 2 kg 505 g or 2.505 kg
21. 3,096
22. 60 seconds; 60 minutes; 7 days; 365 days; 366 days

23. **a)**

Transport	Tally
Car	卌 卌 卌 |||
Walk	卌 卌 ||
Bus	卌 卌 ||||
Bicycle	卌 |||

b) Car
c) 52
24. 20 coins
25. 13:50
26. **a)** 2
b) 3
c) 2
27. **a)** Point A: (3,2); Point B: (5,6)
b) No. To draw an isosceles triangle, you need to plot a point at (7,2).
28. 294 passengers
29. **a)** Scalene triangle
b) All three angles are different sizes; All three sides are different lengths **(Both points for 1 mark)**
30. £612
31. C
32. £21
33.

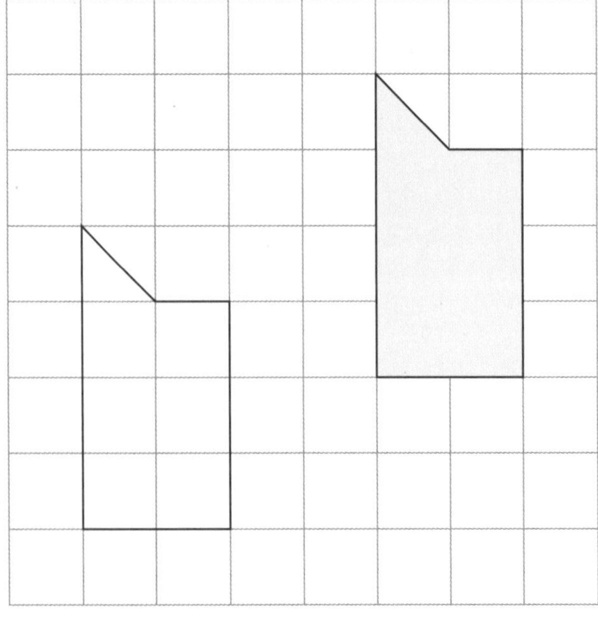

English glossary

Adverbial A word or phrase used to add further information about time or place. Example: in the swimming pool.

Apostrophe A punctuation mark used in two different ways: 1. Showing contraction – replacing missing letters in contracted words; example: I'm = I am; 2. Showing belonging (possession); example: Dad's hat.

Ascender The part of taller letters that rises higher than the main part of the letter. Examples: b, d, h.

Character A person in a story or a poem.

Comma A punctuation mark used to separate items in a list and to show different parts of a sentence.

Composition Putting together a piece of writing.

Conjunction A word used to join two sentences or parts of a sentence. Examples: and, or, if, but, because, that, when.

Convention Common features and techniques used by writers in different genres. Examples: good and evil characters in a fairytale.

Descender The part of letters that extends lower than the main part of the letter. Examples: g, j, p, q.

Determiner A word used to identify nouns by being specific (e.g. that ball, your ball, his ball, the ball) or more general (e.g. a ball)

Dictionary A book containing an alphabetical list of words, with a definition of what each word means and what type of word it is.

Direct speech The exact words spoken aloud by a character in a story.

Editing Making improvements to a piece of writing.

Evidence Words from a text that can be used to justify an idea about the text.

Expanded noun phrase An extension of the part of a sentence containing a noun (e.g. the tree) by adding further detail. Examples: the tall, green tree; the tree in the field.

Fronted adverbial An adverbial used at the start of a sentence. Example: In the swimming pool, we played with a ball.

Glossary An alphabetical list in a non-fiction book, giving key words and their meanings.

Homophones Different words with different spelling that sound the same when spoken.

Inference Using ideas in a text to decide how or why something has happened, or how and why a character acts or feels in a certain way.

Intonation The way words are spoken to enhance or emphasise their meaning.

Inverted commas Special punctuation marks used to show when words spoken in direct speech start and end. Also known as speech marks.

Noun The name of a person, place or thing.

Paragraph A way of structuring text so sentences on the same topic are grouped together. For example, one paragraph may include sentences describing a character and the next paragraph may include sentences about the setting.

Plan The key ideas and sections a text will have. Notes written as part of a plan can then be used to help when writing the text.

Plot What happens in a story.

Poem Writing that expresses ideas of feeling about someone or something, sometimes using rhyming words.

Possessive apostrophe An apostrophe used to show when an object belongs to someone or something. Example: Tom's bike.

Prefix Letters added to the beginning of a root word that change the word's meaning.

Pronoun A word used in place of a noun. Example: she, he, it.

Proofreading Reading through writing to check for sense and mistakes.

Root word A word before any further letters are added that alter the meaning. Example: jump is a root word which can have letters added to become jumper, jumped or jumping.

Setting Where a story or poem takes place, i.e. where it is set.

Suffix Letters added to the end of a root word that change the word's meaning.

Summary Putting the main information or ideas from a text into your own words.

Text features Features common to a type of writing. Example: subheadings in a non-fiction text.

Theme Ideas put across by the author of a text. Examples: kindness, honesty, friendship.

Verb A doing word

Word ending Common letter patterns at the end of words, such as **-sure** (treasure) or **-ture** (picture).

Word origin Where a word comes from. Example: many words contain the **gue** spelling from the French language, e.g. vague, meringue.

Maths glossary

24-hour The 24-hour clock goes from 00:00 (midnight) to 23:59 (one minute to midnight). This is known as 'digital' time.

Acute An angle less than 90°.

Addition To combine two or more numbers together, to make a new number called the sum. Represented by the symbol '+'.

Analogue (clock) 12-hour time written as a.m. (morning) or p.m. (afternoon) usually shown by a clock face with hands.

Angle An amount of turn; measured in degrees.

Area The area of a shape is how much surface it has. Area is measured in square units such as square centimetres (cm^2) and square metres (m^2).

Bar chart A graph that uses bars to show information. The bars are all the same width and can be horizontal or vertical.

Calculate Working out the answer to a number problem.

Capacity How much something holds; usually measured in litres and millilitres.

Carry Moving a digit to the next column in a calculation.

Change When the amount paid was more than the cost.

Check Testing the accuracy of the calculation to make sure it is correct.

Coordinate grid A square grid that shows coordinates.

Coordinates Two numbers or letters that describe a position on a map, grid, graph or chart. The horizontal (x-axis coordinate) is given first and then followed by the vertical (y-axis coordinate).

Column A line of things arranged vertically.

Convert Changing one thing into another. For example, you can convert different measurement units, such as kilograms to grams.

Data Information or facts you find out or are given. Data can be words, numbers, or words and numbers together.

Decimal number A number based on ten, multiples of ten and tenths.

Decimal point A point used to separate whole numbers from decimal fractions.

Degrees The units used to measure angles. Example: a right angle is 90 degrees (90°).

Denominator The bottom part of a fraction, which tells you how many equal parts the whole has been divided into.

Digit There are ten digits – 0, 1, 2, 3, 4, 5, 6, 7, 8 and 9. Digits are used to build other numbers.

Digital (clock) A clock that has only numbers on it.

Division When you share things equally.

Edge (side) Where two faces of a shape meet; can be straight or curved.

Equal Two things are equal if they are the same in some way. Numbers or calculations are equal when they are worth the same.

Equal to (=) The symbol used to show equal quantities or numbers.

Equilateral triangle A triangle with three equal sides and three equal angles.

Equivalent Something that is equal to something else.

Estimate A sensible guess at an answer without doing the calculation.

Exchange To change a number to help complete calculations. Example: changing 40 into 30 and 10, to allow you to move 10 into the ones column.

Factor pairs A set of two numbers we multiply to get a product. Example: 5 and 6 are factors of 30.

Fraction A number that represents part of a whole. Example: $\frac{1}{2}$ or $\frac{1}{4}$.

Frequency How often something happens. Tally marks are often used to show the frequency in a frequency chart or diagram.

Greater than (>) A quantity or number that is larger, when compared against another. Example: 117 > 107.

Horizontal A line that is parallel to the horizon or ground. Example: a table has a horizontal top.

Hour A measurement of time. There are 24 hours in one day. An hour is divided into minutes and seconds. 1 hour = 60 minutes; 1 hour = 3,600 seconds.

Hundred The place value where the digit equals a number of hundreds. Example: 409 has 4 hundreds.

Hundredth A number that has been divided by 100.

Inverse Inverse means to reverse something. Addition and subtraction are inverse operations. Multiplication and division are also inverse operations. The inverse operation undoes the previous calculation.

Irregular (polygon) A polygon with sides of different length and/or angles of different sizes.

Isosceles triangle A triangle with two sides the same length and two equal angles.

Leap year A year occurring once every four years which has 366 days.

Length A measure of the longest side of a shape measured in mm, cm and m.

Less Something that is smaller than something else. Example: 4 is less than 6.

Less than (<) A quantity or number that is smaller, when compared against another. Example: 107 < 117.

Mass How heavy something is; usually recorded in grams or kilograms.

Minute A measurement of time. There are 60 minutes in 1 hour. A minute can be divided up into 60 seconds.

Month A measurement of time; There are twelve months in one year.

More Something that is greater than something else. Example: 10 is more than 4.

Multiple The result of multiplying a given number by any other number. Example: multiples of 4 are 4, 8, 12, 16 ... (the 4 times table answers).

Multiplication Adding lots of the same number together. Represented by the symbol '×'.

Numerator The top number of a fraction, which tells you how many equal parts there are.

Obtuse An angle that measures between 90° and 180°.

One The place value where the digit represents a number of ones.

Order When you put things in order of size or quantity.

Part A fraction of a whole. Example: 5 is the whole, so 3 and 2 are parts of 5.

Pence (p) A value of money. There are 100 pence in £1.

Perimeter The total distance around the outside of a 2-D shape.

Pictogram A graph where pictures or symbols are used to stand for quantities; a picture can stand for one thing or a number of things.

Place value The value of each digit, shown by its position in the number.

Polygon Any 2-D shape with straight sides.

Position The point at where something is located.

Pounds (£) A value of money. £1 is equal to 100 pence.

Product The result of multiplying two or more numbers together. Example: the product of 4 × 6 is 24.

Proper fraction A fraction when the numerator is smaller than the denominator. It is a fraction worth less than 1. Example: $\frac{3}{4}$.

Quadrilateral A four-sided shape. Examples: square, rectangle, trapezium, kite, rhombus, parallelogram

Regular (polygon) Any polygon that has all its sides and angles the same size.

Right angle An angle equalling 90° between two straight lines.

Right-angled triangle A triangle with one angle of 90°.

Roman numeral Letters that the Romans used to stand for numbers.

Rounding Writing a number as an approximate to the nearest whole unit.

Round down Rounding a number down to the nearest whole unit.

Round up Rounding a number up to the nearest whole unit.

Scalene triangle A triangle with no equal sides or angles.

Second A unit of time. There are 60 seconds in 1 minute and 3,600 seconds in an hour.

Straight (angle) A straight angle is a half turn. It is two right angles.

Subtraction To take one number away from another; the difference between two numbers. Subtract is the inverse of add. Represented by the minus symbol '–'.

Symbol A sign used to represent words.

Systematic When things are done in an ordered way.

Table When information is written in an orderly list using rows and columns.

Tally A mark which shows how often something happens.

Ten The place value where that digit represents a number of tens.

Tenth A number that has been divided by 10.

Thousand The place value where the digit equals a number of thousands. Example: 2,409 has 2 thousands (2,000).

Time graph A graph that shows how far an object has travelled over a given amount of time.

Total The sum of numbers, found by adding or subtracting numbers together.

Translate To move a shape to a different position. In a translation you do not turn or rotate the shape.

Triangle A three-sided shape. Examples: scalene, equilateral, isosceles, right-angled.

Turn A movement when an object spins or rotates.

Vertical A line that goes up and down.

Vertices Also known as corner(s). The place on a 3-D shape where 3 faces meet. Also used to describe the corners of a 2-D shape.

Whole number A number that does not have any fraction or decimal parts. Example: 34, 5, 126.

x-axis The horizontal axis of a graph.

y-axis The vertical axis of a graph.

Year A length of time consisting of 365 days.

Acknowledgements

Published by Collins
An imprint of HarperCollins*Publishers*
1 London Bridge Street, London SE1 9GF
HarperCollins*Publishers*
Macken House, 39/40 Mayor Street Upper,
Dublin 1, D01 C9W8, Ireland
ISBN: 978-0-00-839880-4
First published 2020
10 9 8 7 6

British Library Cataloguing in Publication Data.
A CIP record of this book is available from the British Library.
Publisher: Fiona McGlade
Project Development: Katie Galloway
Project Management and Editorial: Charlotte Christensen
Cover Design: Kevin Robbins and Sarah Duxbury
Inside Concept Design: Ian Wrigley
Page Layout: Q2A Media
Production: Karen Nulty
Printed in the United Kingdom by Martins the Printers

Progress charts

Use these charts to record your results in the five Progress Tests. Colour in the questions that you got right to help you identify any areas that you might need to study and practise again. (These areas are indicated in the 'See page…' row in the charts.)

Progress test 1: English

	Q1	Q2	Q3	Q4	Q5	Q6	Q7	Q8	Q9	TOTAL /35
See page…	4	6	8	8	10, 14	12	14	16	18, 14	

Progress test 2: Maths

	Q1	Q2	Q3	Q4	Q5	Q6	Q7	Q8	Q9	Q10	Q11	Q12	Q13	Q14	Q15	Q16	Q17	Q18	Q19	Q20	TOTAL /36
See page…	28	34	26	32	36, 30	34	38, 40	28	28	34, 36	26	38, 40	26	38, 40	28	38	32	34, 36	42	36	

Progress test 3: English

	Q1	Q2	Q3	Q4	Q5	Q6	Q7	Q8	Q9	TOTAL /43
See page…	12	48	48	50	54	52	56	58	62	

Progress test 4: Maths

	Q1	Q2	Q3	Q4	Q5	Q6	Q7	Q8	Q9	Q10	Q11	Q12	Q13	Q14	Q15	Q16	Q17	Q18	Q19	Q20	TOTAL /44
See page…	68	76	78	26	28	34, 78	34, 36	28	68	38	78	68, 72	38	68	26	82	68	70	84	90	

Progress test 5: English

	Q1	Q2	Q3	Q4	Q5	Q6	Q7	Q8	Q9	Q10	Q11	Q12	TOTAL /56
See page…	62	58, 60	6	96	98	100	104	106	104	100	12, 16	8	

Use this table to record your results for the Mixed questions sections on pages 112–125.

English mixed questions	Total score:	/ 65 marks
Maths mixed questions	Total score:	/ 65 marks